CHRISTIANS & JEWS

THE TWO FACES OF ISRAEL!

The Unvailing of the Mysteries of the Kingdom

By

Stephen J Spykerman

PRESS

TABLE OF CONTENTS

are those two sons of the father in this parable? – Are they mentioned elsewhere in the Bible? – What is meant by the father's house and where is its location? – So, what do the pigs signify? – What about the mighty famine, what does it mean? – Why is the Prodigal Son given a new robe by his father? – Why does the father place a ring on the Prodigal's hand? – What is the significance of the sandals placed on his feet? – Why the fatted calf and the great feast? – Why is the older brother angry? – Did the older brother in the parable have a case? – The sole 'SIGN' that identifies – What more can we learn about the older son? – What did the father mean when by saying; "Your brother was dead and is alive again?"

Acknowledgments

First and foremost I acknowledge Abba, my Father in Heaven, to whom I owe all I am and ever will be. I thank Him for His loving and patient ministry towards me these past forty years I have walked with His Son, my Redeemer and Savior. This work is done at His instigation and all honor and glory goes to Him.

Then I also thank my precious wife Virginia for her unfailing loyalty, forebearance and love. She has been a true helpmeet to me, without which this work could not have been done.

My thanks must also go to my daughters Rachel Emma and Melissa Anne for their helpful input and continual encouragement.

The contribution made by my dear friend John Hulley of Jerusalem, to some of the content of Chapter six, also needs to be acknowledged. His research on the subject of the origins of Christian

*Zionism has been of invaluable assistance and I
thank him for his help.*

*Grateful thanks and my deepest appreciation go to
Valerie Baxter who at the last moment stepped into
the breach to help edit this book. I will always be
grateful for the outstanding editing work that was
done by her at such short notice.*

*Finally, I want to pay tribute to Stephen Allen, who,
without his knowledge, gave me the formula for
this work. I thank him in particular for being the
inspiration for the Parable about the Ten Virgins. It
was his treatment of this parable, which led me to
examine all the parables of Jesus (Messiah Yeshua)
in the same light.*

AUTHOR'S TESTIMONY

When, some twelve years ago, I came into the revelation of the prophetic significance of the two distinct Houses of Israel, as revealed in both the Old and the New Testaments of the Bible, I could hardly contain my excitement. The new knowledge spoke deeply into my spirit and it totally transformed my life, as I received a call from the LORD to become a "Watchman on Mount Ephraim" (Jer 31 v 6). In my enthusiasm, I was guilty of making the same mistake of any newly found babe in Christ in passionately wanting to share my new knowledge with almost anyone of my acquaintance. In doing this I found that every Christian sister or brother that I shared with, totally rejected the message and often went on to reject me also. After some years of this response, I found myself getting into a very bad attitude towards Christianity or Christians in general. I went as far as vowing to myself that I would never address this subject to a Christian audience again. Since that time, all the articles and books I have written and all the sermons I have given, have been directed at the 'man in the street' or to Messianic audiences.

I would often publicly comment on my unhappy past experiences with Christians, and state quite categorically that I would never bother with trying to address them in my work.

On one of these occasions, I was immediately stopped in my tracks by the Voice of the Lord, who rebuked me with the words, *"How DARE you write these people off!"* He then instructed me to write a book specifically addressed to a Christian audience.

I confessed my sin of presumption to the Lord, and repented in dust and ashes over my appalling arrogance. The resulting action was this book. My hope is that many Christians will have their lives enriched and transformed by its message. I apologise in advance to any Christian reader who might take offence at anything written in this book, as this is not my intention. Having been firmly rebuked by the Lord, my heart is to serve you and to share with you those things that have been revealed to me.

Stephen J Spykerman

Foreword

*A*new phenomenon has manifested itself inside the
Christian Church. It appears to be a world wide
grass roots spiritual movement which is calling people to
re-examine the Hebrew roots of their faith. This movement
is not well defined yet, it is likely the most significant spiritual event to occur within the Christian Church since the
Charismatic movement of some 45 years ago. This phenomenon is referred to as the "HEBREW ROOTS MOVEMENT"
or the "Messianic Israel Movement."

The focus of this movement involves Christians returning
to a Hebraic expression of the Christian faith. This movement is neither monolithic, well organised, nor is it being
orchestrated by any denomination or group of Christian
leaders. It is strictly grass roots and it is the result of what
appears to be a spontaneous spiritual combustion in the
hearts and minds of Christians who read their Bibles. The
theology and doctrines they have been taught at times seem
to be in contradiction with the Word of God. They have
come to realise that the Christianity of today takes on a very
different expression than from its Hebrew roots. Today's
Christianity is heavily influenced by Emperor Constantine,
the Roman Catholic Church, and the Paganism of its time.
It is very different from that of the first-century Messianic

Jewish Believers, including the twelve apostles of Jesus (Yeshua) and the apostle Paul, as chronicled in the Book of Acts. The followers of this new Hebrew roots movement have concluded that the Protestant Reformation did not go anywhere near far enough to reform the church and they wish to complete the work those 16th century reformers began.

In this book, I intend to introduce some fresh and exciting new interpretations to some of the New Testament Parables and miracles of Christ Jesus (Messiah Yeshua) - interpretations that in the main, were given to me as personal revelations. It is with great joy that I bring these to you, as Jesus (Yeshua the Messiah) says:

"For nothing is hidden, except to be revealed; nor has anything been secret, but that it should come to light. If anyone has ears to hear, let him hear!" (Mark 4:22-23, NASB).

With, 'Christians & Jews – the Two Faces of Israel', I hope to bring an inspiring and new perspective that will help Christians to gain a deeper appreciation of their wonderful calling in Christ, the Messiah. I will seek to open up a truth to both Christian and Jew, as to their origins, which will be especially encouraging to Christians. I will speak of the two Houses of Israel, the House of Ephraim and the House of Judah. I will examine who they were, where they might be now, how this is relevant to our calling in Christ Jesus and how it impacts us in our lives today.

In putting some "flesh on the bones", in the way of scriptural evidence, I will encourage my Christian brothers and sisters to return to their roots; their Hebrew roots, so as to attempt to understand their Jewish Savior, Yeshua (Jesus Christ).

CHAPTER ONE

MEET THE TRUE SHEPHERD OF ISRAEL

☙☙

The lost sheep of the house of Israel

In studying the words of the Bible prophets and Jewish sages we discover that they frequently refer to Israel as being composed of two distinct entities, namely Judah and Israel. Whereas the Bible records their miraculous deliverance and exodus from Egypt as one nation comprised of the twelve tribes of Israel, yet, it goes on to state that the nation after the reign of Solomon became divided into two nations with ten tribes going their separate way. The messianic vision of the prophets speaks of a yet future glorious reunification which is destined to take place in the times of the end, when the two nations will come together again under the reign of Messiah the Son of David.

The author agrees whole heartedly with the prophets of the Bible, the Jewish sages and biblical scholars regarding the fact that the ten tribes of the Northern Kingdom of Israel, (also known as the House of Ephraim, or just as Ephraim) is destined to be reunited with the Southern Kingdom of Judah (also known as the House of Judah) into one nation

15

Gospel of the kingdom [handwritten]

Premise of this book [handwritten]

with Messiah Son of David as the King over both. It is the premise of this book that this is what Messiah Yeshua and His apostles had in their minds eye as they preached the Gospel of the Kingdom.

?? In truth, however, both houses of Israel rebelled against the God of the whole world. All turned to different versions of paganism. All need the redemption and new Light of the Messiah. [handwritten margin notes]

The rebellious ten tribes who seceded from the House of David to set up their own kingdom forsook the God (Elohim) of Israel and the Torah of Moses and turned to paganism. It is for this reason they suffered the ultimate fate of being taken into captivity and transported out of their land and scattered to the outermost parts of the earth. Numerous prophetic pronouncements declare that these same *'lost'* Israelites were one day to be redeemed through the work of Messiah Yeshua, as the Suffering Servant, who we recognise to be none other than Jesus of Nazareth. The Prophets of the Bible declare that those *'lost'* Israelites will be brought back to their spiritual heritage as Israelites in the land of Israel under the righteous rule of Messiah Yeshua (Jesus Christ), the Son of David. This is confirmed by the words of Jesus (Yeshua) in His first incarnation, when He spoke of the reason why His Father had sent Him to the earth:

"I was not sent except to the lost sheep of the house of Israel."
(Matthew 15:24, NKJV)

This agrees very well with what the High Priest Caiaphas acknowledged to the Sanhedrin regarding the death of Jesus Christ:

"You know nothing at all, nor do you consider that it is expedient for us that one man should die for the people, and not that the whole nation should perish (i.e. Judah), and not for that nation only, but also that he would gather together in one the children of God who were scattered abroad (i.e. Ephraim, the lost sheep of the house of Israel). (John 11:50 & 52, NKJV)

It is a fact of life that Christianity as well as the world at large is unaware of the truth that Israel is composed of two separate peoples and nations. The Bible reveals that Israel has two faces with one readily identifiable as Judah, whereas the face of Ephraim/Israel is hidden from view. The ones that are hidden have lost all sense of their Israelite origins and they are indeed the 'lost sheep of the house of Israel.'

Moses in his final message to the children of Israel uttered dire warnings and prophesied what would befall them if they failed to repent from their idolatry and disobedience:

"I said, I would scatter them into corners, I would make the remembrance of them to cease from among men" (Deuteronomy 32:26 KJV).

The prophet Isaiah confirms the words of Moses as he perfectly describes the condition of the house of Israel once they had been expelled from their land:

"The ox knows its owner and the donkey its master's crib; ✳ *but Israel does not know, My people do not consider"* (Isaiah 1:3 NKJV).

The Ox was the tribal standard of the tribe of Ephraim, and it was Ephraim who was the leader of the Northern Kingdom of Israel, which resulted in the term 'Ephraim' becoming the generic name used to describe those ten tribes who seceded from the Davidic Kingdom. The prophet Isaiah is clearly referring here to the sad state of the 'Ox', i.e. the Lost House of Israel, who does not know its owner and who has forgotten where he came from.

The Prophet Daniel was instructed to shut up the words, and seal the book containing the many revelations he had been given until the time of the end. He was told that at that time: **"Many shall run too and fro, and knowledge shall** increase!" Does this sound like the days we are living in today? Think about it! Just a hundred years ago the choice of travel was travel by horse and buggy, or maybe when going long distance, by steam locomotive or ship, whereas today we can reach every part of the globe by jet, and the car is a must for every one allowing us to run to and fro each and every day of our lives. With the invention of computers and the Internet knowledge has increased at a phenomenal rate. Scientist claim that today in the early years of our 21st century, the sum of all human knowledge is doubling every two years and that this trend is accelerating at breakneck speed. However, the term; **"knowledge shall increase"** is a reference not only to the unprecedented explosion of material knowledge but it refers to a similar dramatic unveiling of spiritual knowledge as well. The Prophet Daniel when told to **"shut up the words"** asked again for further revelation as to when the end of these things would be? He was told the following: **"Go your way, Daniel, for the words are closed up and sealed till the time of the end."** (Daniel 12: 4 & 9, NKJV).

Today we live in the days when the seals of the book (the Bible) are being removed and when the words that have been closed up and hidden may finally be revealed and brought out into the open. The revelation that Israel has two faces and is comprised of two distinct nations is part of this process. The 'Good News' is that those two faces are composed of Christians and Jews! This is the time when the veil which the LORD, the God (Elohim) of Israel has placed over the face of the house of Israel will finally be removed. The world will come to marvel at the recognition that Judah has multiple hundreds of millions of Christian relatives, who are his brothers even though they are not Jews. These are the **"the lost sheep of the house of Israel"** which Yeshua (Jesus) had come to save.

The Hebrew Roots Movement, the Messianic Israel Movement, as well as the Christian Zionist movement need to be seen in the context of this prophetic agenda where the Eternal God, the Elohim of Israel, is drawing the two parts of His divided nation to come back together into one United Kingdom again. Essentially, this is what the true Gospel of the Kingdom is all about.

(handwritten: ! / Yes !!)

Meet the Good Shepherd

The prophecies throughout the Book of Ezekiel give us an insight as to how Our Father in Heaven, the Holy One of Israel, views His chosen nation Israel. Ezekiel chapter 34 makes is especially clear that He sees them as a flock of sheep that have been abused and abandoned by her many shepherds. As a result of this negligence, the flock has become scattered over all the earth and no longer dwells as one flock in the land of Israel. This is clearly a most unsatisfactory situation for which the shepherds of Israel are held fully accountable, see verses 4-6. What is the solution to this terrible situation? The answer is given in the same chapter as those abominable shepherds face divine wrath and dismissal:

'Thus says the Lord GOD: "Behold, I am against the shepherds, and I will require My flock at their hand; I will cause them to cease feeding the sheep.......... Indeed I Myself will search for My sheep and seek them out. As a shepherd seeks out his flock on the day he is among his scattered sheep, so will I seek out My sheep and deliver them from all the places where they were scattered....... And I will bring them out from the peoples and gather them from the countries, and will bring them into their own land; I will feed them on the mountains of Israel...." (Ezekiel 34:10-13 NKJV).

(handwritten: At this point, Christianity and its pastors are not interested in being gathered unto Israel and losing their identity)

Since no one was able to re-gather the flock, YHVH Elohim promises to do it Himself. After all, he is the great shepherd of the sheep, as is confirmed by David, the shepherd king of Israel: *"The LORD (YHVH) is my shepherd; I shall not want."* (Psalm 23:1)

How will YHVH shepherd the flock? How will He re-gather His scattered flock? He will do it through His Word, the son of Elohim, the Messiah of Israel. Notice the words of Yeshua:

"I am the good shepherd; and I know My sheep, and am known by My own. As the Father knows Me, even so I know the Father; and I lay down My life for the sheep. And other sheep have I which are not of this fold; them also I must bring, and they will hear My voice; and there will be one flock and one shepherd."
(John 10:14-16 NKJV)

The **"other sheep"** Yeshua mentioned were not part of the Jewish fold He was addressing at the time; rather He was referring to the *"scattered sheep of the Lost House of Israel"*, which are to be found in the Gentile nations of the world. Thus here Yeshua reiterated His mission to re-gather into one flock all of the tribes (Sheep) of Israel. The prophet Ezekiel further emphasises the fact that a large part of Israel's flock has wandered so far and so wide that over the centuries they have simply got lost:

"I will feed My flock, and I will make them lie down," says the Lord GOD. *"I will seek what was lost and bring back what was driven away."* (Ezekiel 34:15-16 NKJV)

The truth is that Judah, as the Jewish people, never got lost. Even during the periods when they were taken into cap-tivity and scattered for a time whilst in the Diaspora, they continued to hold to the Torah and as such they never lost their true origins as the children of Israel. The Jews have always been aware of their Hebrew origins. The whole

Dale

world knows they are the 'chosen' people of God and they have suffered much for it. It is this aspect of their calling that since time immemorial has stuck in the craw of mankind, and hence it has brought so much persecution upon the Jewish people throughout the ages.

The house of Israel on the other hand did get lost and it was those *'lost sheep'* that Ezekiel was referring to. These sheep are blissfully unaware that they are lost and they have no idea that they too are a part of the 'chosen' people of Israel. No idea whatsoever! Notice how these are addressed:

"Thus they shall know that I, the LORD (YHVH) their God, am with them, and they, the house of Israel, are My people," *says the Lord GOD. "You are My flock, the flock of My pasture, you are men, and I am your God," says the Lord GOD.* (Ezekiel 34:30-31 NKJV)

Can we see how the Scripture here emphasises the need to reassure these ignorant sheep of the lost house of Israel? The blindness as to their true heritage is being stripped *Good News!!* away, as at this point in time, *"they shall know that I the LORD their God am with them, and they, of the HOUSE OF ISRAEL, ARE MY PEOPLE. YOU ARE MY FLOCK AND I AM YOUR GOD."* Could this be spelled out in any clearer way? Clearly, this prophetic message by definition cannot be addressed to the Jewish people of the house of Judah, as they already know that the LORD (YHVH) is their God. They are well aware of their election as the *'chosen'* people of GOD and they already know they are the sheep of His pasture. They do not have to be reminded of the fact; yet, those scattered sheep of the house of Israel totally unaware of their *Our Calling* Israelite ancestry do need to have their eyes opened.

This major prophetic event is even now on the horizon, as it is set to happen in our day. For those who have been given the eyes to see, the signs are all around us. In the past twenty five years we have seen a massive move of the Spirit sweeping across the Christian world in which many millions of believers around the world have been given what can only be termed a supernatural love for Israel. Running concurrent with this phenomenon Satan, the adversary of GOD, has orchestrated a global countermove by stoking a massive rise in anti-Semitism. The emergence of the Christian Zionist movement and the phenomenal surge of the Hebrew Roots Restoration movement provide clear evidence that the Holy One of Israel is stirring the Christian world to return to Zion.

The Word of God through the Patriarchs and the Prophets is calling many to *'cross over'* much like Abraham did when he obeyed the call to leave his heritage in the city of Ur, and *'crossed over'* the River Euphrates on his way to the Land of Promise. This is essentially what a Hebrew does, as a Hebrew is one who *'crosses over'* from Babylon into the Land of Promise. It is a work God has already begun in the power and the spirit of Elijah, as millions of believers around the world have been drawn by the Spirit of God to return to their Hebrew roots. The prophet Malachi speaks of this end time phenomenon:

"Behold, I will send you Elijah the prophet before the coming of the great and dreadful day of the LORD. And he will turn the hearts of the fathers to the children and the hearts of the children to the fathers, lest I come and strike the earth with a curse" (Malachi 4:5-6 NKJV).

If we remember to look at this Scripture through the prism of Israel then the fathers being spoken of are clearly the patriarchal fathers of Israel, i.e. Abraham, Isaac and Jacob; whereas the children mentioned here are the seed of Abraham, the children of Israel. The Prophet Isaiah addresses the same theme in:

"You who seek the LORD: Look to the rock from which you were hewn, and to the hole of the pit from which you were dug. Look to Abraham your father, and to Sarah who bore you; for I called him alone, and blessed and increased him" (Isaiah 51:1-2 NKJV).

Increasing numbers of believers are being drawn to recognize the Hebrew roots of their faith with millions around the world keeping the seventh day Sabbath, the Passover and the other Feasts of the LORD (Leviticus 23:1). Thus, perhaps even without knowing it, these believers are looking to: *'the rock from which they were hewn, and to the hole of the pit from which they were dug, unaware that they, being of the seed of Abraham, are being drawn to walk into those ancient paths'.* This prophecy is being fulfilled in our day! For example, one only has to look at those 7,000 believers from all around the world who assembled in Jerusalem last year [2009] to keep the ancient biblical Feast of Tabernacles in solidarity with the Jews, under the auspices of the International Christian Embassy in Jerusalem.

The prophet Jeremiah too laments the fact that the children of Israel have forgotten God, and goes on to say: *"And they have caused themselves to stumble in their ways, from the ANCIENT PATHS"* (Jeremiah 18:15 NKJV, emphasis added). The prophet here is speaking about those same *'lost sheep of Israel,* who have strayed away from the true path as expounded by Moses.

In commanding the observance of His Feast of Tabernacles, GOD in effect designed this special seven day long feast to enable His chosen people to celebrate the establishment of His Kingdom here on this earth in advance each year by way of a special anticipatory re-enactment of the glorious reality to come. The angel Gabriel, when visiting the Virgin Miriam, speaking of the Son she was to conceive, said to her:

"He will be great, and will be called the Son of the Highest; and the Lord God will give Him the THRONE OF HIS FATHER DAVID. AND HE WILL REIGN OVER THE WHOLE HOUSE OF JACOB FOREVER." (Luke 1:32-33 NKJV, emphasis added).

[handwritten margin note: why did we never see or deal fully with this?]

The term *'the whole house of Jacob'* refers to all the tribes descended from the twelve sons of Jacob! Thus even in the announcement of the birth of Yeshua, the angel Gabriel referred to the ultimate restoration of the Whole House of Israel into one flock of sheep. This means that the ancient breach between the House of Judah and the House of Israel will finally be healed. It also means that the breach between Judaism and Christianity will be healed, as Messiah Yeshua, the Good Shepherd, will be King over us all. This essentially is what the Gospel of the Kingdom is all about. The Feast of Tabernacles is the advance celebration of the establishment of His glorious Kingdom. Thus all those observing this festival are a living testimony to the soon coming Kingdom of God.

CHAPTER TWO

THE "CHRISTIAN" WATCHMEN ON THE WALLS OF JERUSALEM

๑\๏

Watchmen on the Walls of Jerusalem

Did you know that the Bible speaks of two kinds of watchman? It is a wonderful end-time phenomenon in the Church that many believers have been given a super-natural love for Israel and the Jews, and it truly can be called a move of the Spirit. Those of us who have experienced this love and interest in the State of Israel, Jerusalem, and all things Jewish, have been given a special affinity with a particular Scripture in Isaiah, which announces the inspired prophecy that:

"I HAVE SET WATCHMEN ON YOUR WALLS, O JERUSALEM; they shall never hold their peace day or night. You who make mention of the LORD, do not keep silent, And give Him no rest till He establishes and till He makes Jerusalem a praise in all the earth" (Isaiah 62:6-7 NKJV).

[handwritten marginal note: this is a step]

[handwritten marginal notes: Hopefully focused the Church turning from its pagan replacement practices and back to Torah so that it can not only pray for Israel but be witness to the Jews to provoke them to jealousy and bring them their Messiah Yeshua.]

This prophecy most certainly has become true in our day, as throughout the world there is a significant awakening within the Church, involving millions of Spirit filled believers who are standing in the gap for Israel. They have become watchmen on the walls of Jerusalem in a global movement of intercession for Israel. This great army of Christian watchmen is engaged day and night 24/7 interceding and praying for the protection of Israel. These watchmen, in fulfillment of Isaiah's prophecy, *never hold their peace day or night!* All night prayer vigils for Israel take place every night of the week all around the world, even in far away places such as China, Japan and South America. Even within the confines of the city of Jerusalem itself, at any given time of the year, hundreds of believers are privately engaged in this divine watchman ministry of intercession. This is a most powerful move of God, which is gathering more and more strength even as the dangers to Israel's existence multiply.

However, were you aware that God's Word refers to two kinds of watchman? You may have heard, or even be familiar with those valiant watchmen on the walls of Jerusalem, but did you realize that a different group of watchmen is mentioned in the Bible? We find this other set of end-time watchmen mentioned in the book of Jeremiah:

"For there shall be a day when THE WATCHMEN WILL CRY ON MOUNT EPHRAIM, 'arise, and let us go up to Zion, to the LORD our God'" (Jer.31:6 NKJV).

Now what on earth does this mean? "Mount" in biblical Hebrew usually refers to "nation." However, "Mount Ephraim" implies "Nations" (plural). Ephraim, (the leading tribe) is frequently used in the Bible in its generic context to describe the Lost Ten Tribes of Israel; and having been scattered to the four corners of the earth these tribes consist of many nations.

26

If this is true, it should be very convicting because the Christian Church has FAILED to be a watchman on the wall for truth, Torah, and the fullness of Messiah for over 2,000 yrs. ??

CHRISTIANS & JEWS - THE TWO FACES OF ISRAEL

In Modern day Hebrew the word 'Watch-man' means Christian!

Did you realize that the word for Christians in Modern Hebrew is *Notzrim*? At the same time the word "Watchman" or "Watchmen" are variously derived from three ancient Hebrew words, respectively; *Shamar; Tsaphah & Natsar,* all of them share the same root of *'to guard'.* Is this not amazing? Here we have Isaiah, the son of Amos, prophesying some 2,700 years ago that in our time there would be, *"watchmen on the walls of Jerusalem",* and the word he uses to describe those watchmen happens to be *"Notzrim",* in modern day Hebrew, which is the very term used by the Jewish people to describe *Christians* today! This is even more remarkable when we realize that Modern Hebrew is very different from the Hebrew used in Bible times, as in Isaiah's day the word Christian had never been heard of and therefore the association between Notzrim and Christian did not exist at the time he spoke those words. Below we will also examine Isaiah's reference to; *"the Branch which comes out of the root of Jesse"* In Is. 11:1, the reference to *"the Branch"* is derived from the word *"Netzer",* which comes from the same root word *"Natzar"* e.g. *"watchman!"*

This is quite significant. It means that just prior to the advent of the Messianic Era, when Isaiah's prophecy was to come to pass, saying that there would be *Watchmen on the Walls of Jerusalem,* he was pointing out something that only God could have known. On the other hand, the word for 'watchmen' in Isaiah 62:6 is the Hebrew *'shamarim'* which is related to the word for Samaria. Now, Samaria was the ancient capital of the Northern Kingdom of Israel which rules over the ten tribes of Israel who had separated themselves from Judah and the house of David. Thus even in this we have an indication that the prophet is referring to Ephraim, those from the rebellious house of Israel. Furthermore, both words have the same root *'shamar'*, *meaning 'to watch' and* *'guard'.* As we see that the word 'Notzrim' is taken from Modern day Hebrew, the words of Isaiah may reasonably be taken to apply to those modern day Christians who love the modern day State of Israel. The primary commission of the watchmen on the walls of Jerusalem is one of fervent intercession for the present Jewish State of Israel. However, the other set of watchmen referred to by the prophet Jeremiah have a completely different job to do. **The role of those watchmen is to:**

"Cry on Mount Ephraim; 'Arise, and let us go up to Zion, to the LORD our God'" (Jeremiah 31:6 NKJV).

Their commission is to preach the Gospel of the Kingdom, which is the same Good News Yeshua and His disciples preached. This Gospel concerns the restoration of the Whole House of Israel into a restored and newly United Kingdom of Israel, which will comprise all of the Twelve Tribes of Israel. It is the advance news about the glorious reign of Messiah Yeshua, who is destined to rule as King of kings and Lord of lords, from the throne of David in Mount Zion. **This means the establishment of God's Kingdom here upon the earth!** Only then will the two faces/halves of Israel become reunited and reconciled with each other. It is by preaching this Good News about the Reunification of the Two Houses of Israel into One United Kingdom that those watchmen on Mount Ephraim will be stirring their fellow tribesmen to return to Zion and the Promised Land. To date this Gospel has largely not been preached, yet we have the assurance from the prophet that Notzrim e.g. Christian Watchmen will be calling upon the tribes of Israel to return to Zion! Thus Jeremiah too was prophesying that the Lost Ten Tribes, in the latter times, would be Christians and Messianic believers. God is even now calling upon those Notzrim/watchmen on Mount Ephraim to begin their kingdom work of calling their fellow Christian tribesmen to return to Zion. Might you be one of these? This means that many in the Church need to follow those who have already returned to those ancient paths, and return to the true Hebrew roots of their faith.

Restoring the Preserved Ones of Israel

The Modern Hebrew word *Notzrim, i.e. the watchmen or Christians,* is derived from the word *Nazareth.* We all know that *Yeshua* (Jesus) was from Nazareth and that He was called the Nazarene. Here lies an amazing hidden relationship between Yeshua and his followers of both Jewish and Gentile believers. No one would have been aware of this relationship until the birth and ministry of Yeshua the Messiah, as prior to His coming it's meaning would have had no particular significance. However, when we examine it's meaning today with the benefit of hindsight, we can discover a most wonderful truth. To get the whole picture we need to first of all go to another passage in the book of Isaiah where the same root word is used:

"It is too small a thing that You should be My Servant to raise up the tribes of Jacob, and to RESTORE THE PRESERVED ONES OF ISRAEL; I will also give You as a light to the Gentiles, that You should be My salvation (Heb.: Yeshua) to the ends of the earth" (Isaiah 49:6 NKJV).

The use of the above phrase, *'restore the preserved ones of Israel',* may well be taken to imply the full and final restoration of Ephraim and the Lost Nations/House of Israel. The remarkable fact is that in the Hebrew the term, *'PRESERVED' ones of Israel,* has the same root word *'NOTZRI' i.*e. Christian or watchman. Thus here we have the Prophet Isaiah using a word that was not used before his time at all, and yet it is the Hebrew word used to describe Christians today! Is this not amazing? This truly reflects the signature of our Creator God! It is translated as the *"preserved of Israel"* in English, whereas elsewhere it is translated *"watchmen"*. Let us now read the Scripture again by injecting this interpretation into Isaiah 49:6:*"to raise up the tribes of Jacob, and to restore the watchmen of Israel (restore the modern day Christian believers who love Israel); I will give you also as a light to the Gentiles,"* etc. It is these Christian watchmen that have been *concealed and hidden*, and they indeed are *the preserved ones of Israel!* Can we see it now? Oh, how wonderful is our GOD!!!

All that remains now is for us to go back to Nazareth in order to conclude our research into those Christian watchmen. Once again we find the key to its remarkable meaning in the book of Isaiah. The Prophet Isaiah in another chapter, when speaking in the context of how the LORD will recover the remnant of His people and assemble the outcasts of Israel, introduces the subject as follows:

A Branch shall grow out of his roots

"There shall come forth a Rod (shoot) from the Stem of Jesse, and a Branch, (netzer, notzrim, watchman), shall grow out of his roots" (Isaiah 11:1 NKJV).

The stem *(Geza in Hebrew)* of Jesse referred to here represents a cut down trunk or stump of a tree, and out of it a shoot *(a wild growth)* comes forth, that is to say out of Jesse, a *"BRANCH"* *(Hebrew: Netzer)* grows out of his roots. In Strong's No: 5342 *'netzer'* is defined as derived from *'natzar'* mentioned in No: 5341. *Netzer* represents *a green (living) shoot'; a descendant: - branch.* Notice that the stem of the tree is above the ground, whereas the roots are underground.

Whilst the stem, trunk or stump of a tree is visible, the roots invariably are invisible and hidden. Remember, that we are looking at God's Word through the prism of Israel. The Stem of Jesse is clearly a reference to Judah, as Judah, much like the trunk of a tree, has always remained visible and above the ground. Now suddenly a *living* (green) *'Rod'*, *'Shoot'* and a *'Branch'* springs up from the roots beneath the ground. This *living Rod, Shoot or Branch* is none other than the Lost House of Israel that has remained underground and hidden for the past three thousand years!

As most prophecies frequently have a <u>dual application</u>, it needs to be said that the conventional interpretation of *The* (living green) *'Branch'* or *'Netzer'* is that it is a reference to Yeshua our Messiah, who was raised up by His human parents in the little town of Netzeret, e.g. (Nazareth) the city of The "BRANCH". This is based upon a number of Messianic Scriptures, a most excellent example of which may be found in the Book of Jeremiah: *"Behold, the days are coming," says the LORD, "That I WILL RAISE TO DAVID A BRANCH OF RIGHTEOUSNESS; a King shall reign and prosper, And execute judgment and righteousness in the earth. In His days JUDAH WILL BE SAVED AND ISRAEL WILL DWELL SAFELY"* (Jeremiah 23:5-6 NKJV). When He, Yeshua, the Messiah, came to His own as the Passover Lamb of God, He expressed the reason why He had been sent by His Father by saying:

"I was not sent except to the lost sheep of the house of Israel"
(Matthew 15:24 NKJV).

By the above words we see that Yeshua was well aware of that *'shoot' or 'branch' or 'descendants'*, *which* being still hidden from view, whilst dwelling underground with the roots, would one day suddenly spring forth into view. He, as the *anointed forerunner* had come to lay down His life in order to save those *Lost Sheep of the House of Israel.* He in fact was the ultimate *shoot* from the stem of Jesse, as He was from the royal lineage of David, as well as being of the House of Judah. The Jews came to refer to Him as the Nazarene, that is to say: **the Branch from the city of the Branch.** He was the leading *'Netzer/Branch'; th*e ultimate *'Notzrim/ Christian,'* as well as the most powerful, influential and diligent *'Watchman, Intercessor'* of all time. Hallelujah! Yet, the story does not end here, as when He commissioned His own disciples He commanded them as follows:

"Do not go into the way of the Gentiles, and do not enter a city of the Samaritans. But GO RATHER TO THE LOST SHEEP OF THE HOUSE OF ISRAEL. And as you go, preach, saying, THE KINGDOM OF HEAVEN IS AT HAND!"
(Matthew 10:5-7 NKJV, emphasis added).

Thus He gave His disciples, the twelve Apostles, the same commission His Father had given Him, as they too were to bring the Good News of the Kingdom to those *"Lost sheep of the house of Israel"* Notice, how Yeshua strictly forbade them from going to the Gentiles or indeed to the Samaritans, their role was to emulate their Master as the first Notzrim or Watchman on Mount Ephraim, alerting the lost and scattered sheep of Israel, that the King Messiah had sent them to give them the Good News that the Kingdom of Israel would be restored. They were not only to proclaim the joyful message that the kingdom of Israel would be restored but also that that very Kingdom of Heaven was now at hand.

CHAPTER THREE

THE PARABLE OF THE PRODIGAL SON

Remember the parable of the Prodigal son?

Most Christians are familiar with the parable of the 'Prodigal Son,' which is seen as a wonderful illustration of the mercy and forgiveness of God, Our Father in Heaven. Yeshua in His parable of the 'Prodigal Son' in Luke 15:11-32 speaks of a certain man who had two sons. His younger son asks to be given his inheritance, only to go away to a far country and waste his inherited fortune on riotous living. After living a lifestyle of self indulgent idolatry and the pursuit of personal pleasure and abandon he ends up totally destitute. This is the very moment a mighty famine arises in his land of exile and he is forced to take a job looking after another mans pigs! His hunger is so acute that he would have gladly filled his stomach with the husks that are fed to the swine, but no one gives him anything to eat. As he is literally perishing with hunger the prodigal son remembers how good things were when he was still in his father's house and his heart turns toward home. Overwhelmed with remorse he becomes convicted of his sin. Utterly humbled by his dire circumstances he repents of his wayward lifestyle and decides to return to his father's house. His heart is filled with shame, as he recognizes that he has rejected his father and disgraced his family name. As he takes the first steps on his journey home he decides that he is not worthy to bear his father name any longer or to be called his son. Instead he resolves to ask his father if he can forgive him and take him on as one of his hired workers instead. As he approaches his fathers land, his father sees him coming from some considerable distance and runs towards him, falling on his neck and kissing him. The son then exclaims:

"Father, I have sinned against heaven and in your sight, and am no longer worthy to be called your son. But the father said to his servants, 'Bring out the best robe and put it on him, and put a ring on his hand and sandals on his feet. 'And bring the fatted calf here and kill it, and let us eat and be merry; 'for this my son was dead and is alive again, he was lost and is found.'" (Luke 15:22-24 NKJV).

His father orders the fatted calf to be slaughtered and makes a great feast for his prodigal son. The story then goes on to relate that the faithful son, who had remained faithful and stayed at home with his father, was upset and would not join the party. The parable continues by relating the father's words to the older son:

"Son, you are always with me, and all that I have is yours. It was right that we should make merry and be glad, for your brother was dead and is alive again, and was lost and is found!" (Luke 15:31-32 NKJV).

Christian interpretation

The Christian interpretation of this parable is that it highlights the infinite mercy of God the Father towards the repentant sinner. The two sons being spoken of are two born again Christian believers. The younger son is attracted by the 'cares of this world' and is tempted to leave his fathers house (the Church) to pursue a life of earthly pleasures, whilst the older son holds faithful to his calling and remains at home serving his father.

The prodigal son recklessly squanders his father's inheritance in riotous living and ends up destitute. He is forced to support himself in the meanest job possible; having to feed another man's pigs. Then a further calamity strikes as the land is afflicted by a severe famine and now his very life is in peril. Having no way out and with his back against the wall he finally recognizes the folly of his ways. With a heart full of repentance he decides to go back to his father's house. As he sets out on his long journey hungry, unwashed, unshaven, with his clothes in tatters, and smelling of pigs he considers that he is no more worthy to be called his father's son. The wonder of this parable is that his father had been looking out for him all the time, He saw him coming from a great way off and ran to greet him with hugs and kisses, this despite his sons filthy state and the overwhelming smell of pigs which hung all over him.

The moral of the parable appears to be that it does not matter what sins we have committed, or indeed what state we are in, there is always a way back to the father for the repentant sinner, as Jesus Christ (Messiah Yeshua), has paid the price for our sins on the cross. The apostle Paul makes this very clear, as he states:

"But God demonstrates His own love toward us, in that while we were still sinners, Christ died for us" (Romans 5:8 NKJV).

An obvious connection with the Prodigal son is found in the Parable of the Lost Sheep which Yeshua relates in the same chapter, as He addresses a great crowd of tax collectors and sinners in Luke 15:4-7:

"What man of you, having a hundred sheep, if he loses one of them, does he not leave the ninety-nine in the wilderness, and go after the one which is lost till he finds it? And when he has found it, he lays it on his shoulders, rejoicing. And when he comes home, he calls to his friends and neighbors, saying to them, 'Rejoice with me, for I have found my sheep which was lost!'" I say to you that likewise there will be more joy in heaven over one sinner who repents than over ninety-nine just persons who need no repentance."

It appears from the above that the core message of the parable is that there is always a way back for the sinner who is lost, and that the way back to the fathers house is through repentance and an absolute belief in the saving sacrifice of Jesus Christ on the cross. The truth is that we are *"saved by grace,"* but we need to remember that it is also true that we are saved by grace because we have *"repented".* Clearly, this is a most important revelation of the Father's heart, which rings absolutely true. The question I want to pose here is this: did Yeshua mean to convey only this to His disciples?

As the Scriptures generally have several layers of meaning, the question we need to ask ourselves is what if there is still more to this parable than we understand on the surface? Might there be yet another message hidden from our view?

What else did Yeshua really intend to convey to His disciples? Let's look at it again as it might just be terribly important. What was really on His heart when He told them this parable? To get to the full meaning Yeshua was trying to convey we will need to adopt a Hebrew mindset as we re-examine the parable.

What was on Yeshua's mind when He gave this parable?

To discover the full meaning of the parable we need to discover what was on Yeshua's mind when He gave this parable to His disciples. We have already covered in chapter one that Yeshua spoke about His other sheep which were not of the fold of Judah. (John 10:15). Then we can understand from Luke 8: 9-10, that Yeshua spoke in parables in order to hide the truth! This seems absolutely incredible to most Christian believers but our Messiah nevertheless made it very clear, as speaking to His disciples He said:

"To you it has been given to know the mysteries of the kingdom of God, but to the rest it is given in parables, that:

'Seeing they may not see, and hearing they may not understand.'
(Luke 8:9-10 NKJV).

In view of the above it is more than probable that Yeshua was addressing a subject that was only familiar to His inner circle. It was only His close disciples who were given to understand the *'mysteries of the Kingdom of God.'* In this term we are given a vital clue, as this parable, much like most of His other parables, was related to the Kingdom of God.

We can find out quite a lot about what was most important to Yeshua's mind, by examining the Gospel He preached:

"And Jesus, went about all Galilee, teaching in their synagogues, preaching the GOSPEL OF THE KINGDOM (Matthew 4:23 NKJV).

Yeshua also showed us where His heart truly was when He gave us His model prayer:

"Our Father which art in heaven, Hallowed be thy name. THY KINGDOM COME, Thy will be done in earth as it is in heaven" (Matthew 6:9-10 KJV).

What is this Kingdom Yeshua speaks of? The kingdom He is referring to is none other than the United Kingdom of Israel over which He is destined to rule as King of Kings and Lord of Lords. It is only when His Kingdom is established upon the earth that the Father's will, will finally be done on earth as it is in heaven! What we need to understand is that this Kingdom is Israel! YHVH, the GOD of ISRAEL'S Divine plan calls for the restoration of the Whole House of Israel, which is the desire of our Messiah's heart. This is confirmed by Yeshua's exhortation to His disciples in verse 33 of the same chapter with a: *"Seek ye first THE KINGDOM OF GOD!"*

The Apostle Paul too: *"Solemnly testified of the kingdom of God,"* and as he dwelt in his rented house in Rome he received all who came to him: *"Preaching the kingdom of God"* (Acts 28:23 & 31 NKJV). As Paul was preaching about the kingdom of God, he was in effect proclaiming the messianic vision of the Restoration of the Kingdom of Israel.

Therefore, the hidden meaning of the parable can only be revealed to those who have that same Messianic Hebrew vision of the restoration of the Kingdom of God. Furthermore, the mysteries of the Kingdom of God can be opened up only to those who have a Hebrew mindset. This mindset can only be acquired by obtaining a good knowledge of the history of Israel, and for this we need to study Israel's history book.

The Bible is Israel's history book

Most believers accept that the Bible is a revelation about the Creator God, which has become the foundation for the beliefs of the two major monotheistic religions of the world that recognize the God of Israel: Judaism and Christianity. What is not generally appreciated is that the Bible, at the same time, is also the most accurate and unbiased history book in the world. In its pages we find a record of the history of only one nation and people. Maybe you have not thought of it in this way before, but Israel is the central focus of the Scriptures, and it is around this one nation and people that absolutely everything in its text revolves. Other nations or peoples mentioned in the Bible only feature as they come into contact with Israel. Thus the Bible can well and truly be called *Israel's History Book*. The Scripture refers to the nation of Israel some 2583 times. This alone demonstrates the paramount importance God attaches to His chosen nation. The Church has an unfortunate history of replacement theology going back for nearly 2000 years in which the central importance of Israel has been marginalized. The place of God's chosen nation has thus been sidelined, if not edited out of the picture altogether. Nevertheless, Israel is what the Bible is all about, and if we are to understand the Word of God, or indeed the parables of Yeshua, His only begotten Son, then we need to look at them through the prism of Israel.

This also means that if we really are seekers after truth then we need to be become familiar with the whole book, and not just devote our time to the New Testament. Most Bible scholars will readily accept that the New Testament cannot be understood without a thorough knowledge of the Old Testament. It follows therefore that the Parables of

Yeshua can never reveal their hidden meaning regarding the *'Mysteries of the Kingdom of God'* without us having at the same time a comprehensive knowledge of the history of Israel.

Israel is the apple of God's eye

We need to be mindful that our Father in Heaven refers to Himself as the God of Israel.

"Then you shall say to Pharaoh, 'Thus says the LORD: "Israel is My son, My firstborn." (Exodus 4:22 NKJV).

Our Almighty Creator God thus identifies Himself as the Father of Israel, and in speaking to Moses on Mount Sinai, He said:

'Now therefore, if you will indeed obey My voice and keep My covenant, then you shall be a special treasure to Me above all people; for all the earth is Mine. 'And you shall be to Me a kingdom of priests and a holy nation.' These are the words which you shall speak to the children of Israel" (Exodus 19:5-6 NKJV).

This is a foundational Scripture as Israel's ultimate destiny is to become a kingdom of priests and a holy nation. In fact in this we are given a prophecy of the Messianic Kingdom that is to come at a yet future time when Israel's destiny is fulfilled. The Gospel of the Kingdom which Yeshua and His disciples, including the Apostle Paul, preached was essentially about the establishment of this same kingdom.

The divine covenant the Bible speaks of is made with only one nation.......

"I have made a covenant with you and with Israel." (Exodus 34:27 NKJV).

After Moses was given the text for the Aaronic blessing by the Almighty Elohim, he was given the concluding verse as follows:

"So they shall put My Name on the children of Israel, and I will bless them."
(Numbers 6:27)

Thus the Creator of the Universe and Author of All Life has placed His Eternal Name upon His chosen people Israel. Thus the LORD (YHVH the Elohim) of Israel made an irreversible decision that can **never** be changed, as He stated:

"For I am the LORD, I do not change!" (Malachi 3:6 NKJV).

King David in his Psalms frequently refers to God as *'The Holy One of Israel.'*

"To You I will sing with the harp, O Holy One of Israel." (Psalms 71:22 NKJV).

One of the most amazing divine declarations of God's love for his people is made by Moses in his final words to the children of Israel just prior to his death:

"For the LORD'S portion is His people; Jacob is the place of His inheritance. "He found him in a desert land, and in the wasteland, a howling wilderness; He encircled him, He instructed him, He kept him as the apple of His eye."
(Deuteronomy 32:9-10 NKJV).

41

When we look at all of this scriptural evidence we can see that God's heart is focused on His people, the children of Israel. Israel is His nation! The Israelites and all their descendants are His chosen people. Everything God does and whatever He speaks has therefore to be seen in the light of Israel. The same goes for Messiah Yeshua, His only begotten Son. Yeshua does not have a different approach to His Father, as He made the following statements to His disciples:

"He who has seen Me has seen the Father; so how can you say show us the Father? Do you not believe that I am in the Father, and the Father in Me? The words that I speak to you I do not speak on My own authority; but the Father who dwells in Me does the works." (John 14:9b-10 NKJV).

"But that the world may know that I love the Father, and as the Father gave Me commandment, so do I." (John 15:31 NKJV).

Thus if the Father's love and concern is wholly focused upon His chosen nation Israel, we can expect His Son to have the same overriding concern. In this we are given a vital key in unlocking the *Mystery of the Kingdom of God*, whose secret code Yeshua hid in His parables. This key is the realization that the parables are essentially about Israel and her future destiny. The primary purpose of the parables therefore is not to convey some moral lesson or truth, although most of them indeed do so, but rather to give a prophecy about Israel's future restoration.

Who is the father of the Prodigal Son?

The first thing we need to realize is that this parable is about Israel. The father being spoken of is none other that God the Father, the Holy One of Israel. Remember, Israel is His firstborn son whose destiny is to become a kingdom of priests and a holy nation, He has made a covenant with her and placed His Name upon her, and she is the apple of His eye.

A terrible breach has occurred

Sadly a spirit of rebellion has taken hold of His people and consequently a terrible breach has taken place. His nation Israel which was comprised of twelve tribes became a divided kingdom. The breach occurred after the reign of King Solomon, when ten tribes rebelled against the divine order, to set up their own kingdom to the north of Jerusalem. The rump of the original kingdom was centered on Jerusalem and it took the name of Judah after its leading tribe, whereas the ten tribes which seceded from the House of David applied the name Israel with Samaria as their new capital. We thus see Israel divided into two kingdoms, one called Judah and the other Israel. This sad divorce between the tribes of Israel has been faithfully recorded for us in; 1Kings 12: 1-33. Ever since that time the Bible, Israel's history book, has referred to the former United Davidic Kingdom of Israel, as the Kingdom/ House of Judah, and the Kingdom or House of Israel, with each nation following its own path. They have remained totally separate entities ever since the division occurred some three thousand years ago. When we understand this historic fact we have uncovered one of the most important keys to understanding the prophecies of the Bible.

Who are those two sons of the father in this parable?

It is only as we understand what happened to Israel way back then that we can begin to comprehend what Yeshua was getting at when He referred to a father with two sons. Remember, He is the Father of Israel as Israel is His firstborn son. The father in the parable therefore is none other than

God the Father, the Holy One of Israel. Thus when Israel divides into two kingdoms, the Father acquires two sons, and it is these two sons, one called Judah and the other called Israel, who now represent the new reality. The allegorical interpretation is that of a father who had two sons, e.g. one representing the unfaithful/prodigal House of Israel and the other the faithful House of Judah, as only Judah, as represented by the Jewish people, has largely remained faithful to the Torah, the statutes and ordinances of the Holy One of Israel. The ten tribes of the House of Israel on the other hand broke their covenant with YHVH, the God of Israel and went headlong into paganism and idolatry.

Are they mentioned elsewhere in the Bible?

Yes, hundreds of times, especially in the prophets! Furthermore, the separation between the House of Judah and the House of Israel is amply recorded both in the historical books of Kings and Chronicles. This tragic divorce occurred in the first year of the reign of King Rehoboam, who succeeded his father Solomon in 930 BC. Thus over three thousand years ago Israel was split into two kingdoms. You can read all about it in Israel's history book in 1 Kings, the 11th and 12th chapters. Ever since that day the books of Kings and Chronicles have recorded the separate histories of the two kingdoms including the kings' list of the respective royal dynasties ruling over them. The Bible also records several occasions when Judah and Israel go to war against each other. In one such incident the Scriptures even speak of a king of Israel taking the king of Judah captive and sacking Jerusalem! Israel's history books records the event as follows:

"But Amaziah would not heed. Therefore Jehoash king of Israel went out; so he and Amaziah king of Judah faced one another at Beth Shemesh, which belongs to Judah.

And Judah was defeated by Israel, and every man fled to his tent. Then Jehoash king of Israel captured Amaziah king of Judah, the son of Jehoash, the son of Ahaziah, at Beth Shemesh; and he went to Jerusalem, and broke down the wall of Jerusalem from the Gate of Ephraim to the Corner gate-four hundred cubits. And he took all the gold and silver, all the articles that were found in the house of the LORD and in the treasuries of the king's house, and hostages, and returned to Samaria."
(2 Kings 14:11-14 NKJV).

Ever since the separation occurred the prophets of Israel have been speaking of the day when the two nations will come together again. 'The' major prophetic theme of the prophets of the Bible is the ultimate restoration of the two houses of Israel into one United Kingdom. Even the apostle Peter referred to this restoration when he addressed his countrymen from the house of Judah in Solomon's Porch:

"Repent ye therefore, and be converted, that your sins may be blotted out, when the times of refreshing shall come from the presence of the LORD; And he shall send Jesus Christ, which before was preached unto you: Whom the heaven must receive until the times of restitution of all things which God hath spoken by the mouth of all his holy prophets since the world began." (Acts 3:19-21 KJV).

Restitution means restoring to a former state or condition and it is speaking here about the restoration of God's government on the earth through His nation Israel. Peter goes on in verse 22 to refer to the words of Moses who spoke about the Messiah to come as follows:

"The LORD your God will raise up for you a Prophet like me from your midst, from your brethren, Him you shall hear" (Deuteronomy 18:15 NKJV).

To summarize Judah and Israel, the two sons of the Father, are most certainly mentioned in the Bible, and it may well be said that the whole of God's Word revolves around those two.

What is meant by the father's house and where is its location?

The father's house is a reference to the Land of Israel. As the Scripture says:

"The land shall not be sold permanently, for the land is Mine; for you are strangers and sojourners with Me" (Leviticus 25:23 NKJV).

It is also in the Land of Israel where King Solomon was commissioned by the God of Israel to build the Temple of the LORD:

"And it came to pass, when Solomon had finished building the house of the LORD......... that the LORD appeared to Solomon the second time, as He had appeared to him at Gibeon. And the LORD said to him: "I have heard your prayer and your supplication that you have made before Me; I have consecrated this house which you have built to put My Name there forever, and My eyes and My heart will be there perpetually." (1 Kings 9:1-3 NKJV).

The father's house clearly is in the place where the Eternal Father of Israel placed His name and where He had His house. Thus in using the term the *'house of the father'* in the parable Messiah Yeshua is speaking about the land of Israel. In fact the little strip of land on the Mediterranean coast presently occupied by the State of Israel is as nothing to the land God promised to Abraham by an eternal covenant.

"On the same day the LORD made a covenant with Abram, saying: "To your descendants I have given this land, from the river of Egypt to the great river, the River Euphrates." (Genesis 15:18 NKJV).

In the days of King Solomon this promise had its initial fulfillment, as the writ of Solomon stretched all the way from the River Nile in Egypt to the River Euphrates in present day Iraq. During his reign Israel experienced forty years of peace and a time of exceptional prosperity. The Sages of Israel consider his reign to have been but a small foretaste of the millennial era that is to be ushered in by the Messiah of Israel. All of this extra land promised to the descendants of Abraham will surely be needed when the multiple millions of the prodigal ten tribes of Israel return to the father's house to join their brother Judah.

Why does the Prodigal son leave his fathers house?

It was his rebellion against the covenant which caused prodigal Israel to be expelled from the land. Subsequent to their separation from Judah, the ten seceding tribes of Israel, led by the tribe of Ephraim, departed from the Torah. Their king Jeroboam set up golden calves for his people to worship and led the nation headlong into idolatry and hedonistic materialism. In His love for His chosen people God sent many prophets to warn them of the consequences of their sins, yet all to no avail, as the rebellious House of Israel refused to heed the multiple warnings given. Those prophets over and again listed all the curses for disobedience enumerated by Moses in the book of Deuteronomy, but Israel simply would not listen.

"Moreover all these curses shall come upon you and pursue and overtake you, until you are destroyed, because you did not obey the voice of the LORD your God, to keep His commandments and His statutes which He commanded you. "And they shall be upon you for a sign and a wonder, and on your descendants forever. "because you did not serve the LORD your God with joy and gladness of heart, for the abundance of everything, "therefore you shall serve your enemies, whom the LORD will send against you, in hunger, in thirst, in nakedness, and in need of everything; and He will put a yoke of iron on your neck until He has destroyed you. "The LORD will bring a nation against you from afar, from the ends of the earth, as swift as the eagle flies, a nation whose language you will not understand, "a nation of fierce countenance, which does not respect the elderly nor show favor to the young." (Deuteronomy 28:45-50 NKJV).

Moses words and the stark prophetic warnings they contained eventually came to pass as the fearful Assyrian Empire assailed the Kingdom of Israel in three successive invasions. Each time a large section of the Israelite population was taken away and deported to the northern most reaches of their empire. The final deportation took place at the end of a three year siege of the capital city of Samaria in 721 BC.

Thus the ultimate sanction for disobedience which Moses had outlined to the children of Israel finally came into effect after they had rejected and ignored all the warnings of the prophets of Israel for nearly 200 years.

"And it shall be, that just as the LORD rejoiced over you to do you good and multiply you, so the LORD will rejoice

over you to destroy you and bring you to nothing; and you
shall be plucked from off the land which you go to possess.
"Then the LORD will scatter you among all the peoples,
from one end of the earth to the other, and there you shall
serve other gods." (Deuteronomy 28:63-64 NKJV).

This is how the Prodigal House of Israel ended up in
a far country miles away from his fathers house, where he
wasted his spiritual inheritance with prodigal living. Judah
was the elder son of the father in the Parable, whereas Israel,
who was led by Ephraim, the younger son of Joseph, was
the younger son who left his father's house. The truth is that
ever since the two houses of Israel have been apart it has
been the Father's intention one day to bring the two houses
together into one nation and one kingdom once again. This
is essentially what the Gospel of the Kingdom is all about,
as the Father heart of the God of Israel yearns for the time
when His nation will be restored into One United Kingdom
once again. In this parable Yeshua, as the future King of
that restored Kingdom, is thus prophesying that the modern
day descendants of those ten northern tribes of Israel, which
were taken into captivity by the Assyrians in 721BC, will
one day return to their ancestral home in the land of Israel.

Why does the prodigal son leave his father's house?
Well, the answer is that it was his spirit of rebellion and his
involvement into the occult that caused him to be removed
by force. The prodigal son was simply reaping what he had
sown and he was expelled from the land and scattered among
the nations even to the ends of the earth.

So, what then do the pigs signify?

Every word of Messiah Yeshua in this parable has a
deep significance, and so it is with His reference to the pigs.
The prodigal son ended up in a far away land where he was

forced to tend to another man's pigs. What can this possibly mean? The Word of God always interprets itself and we find the answer in the Scriptures:

Now the LORD spoke to Moses and Aaron, saying to them, "Speak to the children of Israel, saying, 'These are the animals which you may eat among all the animals that are on the earth: 'Among the animals, whatever divides the hoof, having cloven hooves and chewing the cud—that you may eat, 'and the swine, though it divides the hoof, having cloven hooves, yet does not chew the cud, is unclean to you. 'Their flesh you shall not eat, and their carcasses you shall not touch. They are unclean to you."
(Leviticus 11:1-3 & 7 NKJV).

In the previous chapter we find a most significant statement which puts the above Divine health law in perfect context:

"That you may distinguish between holy and unholy, and between unclean and clean, and that you may teach the children of Israel all the statutes which the LORD has spoken to them by the hand of Moses." (Leviticus 10:10-11 NKJV).

A thousand years before Moses, Noah was asked to take seven clean animals and only two unclean animals on board the ark:

"You shall take with you seven each of every clean animal, a male and his female; two each of animals that are unclean." (Genesis 7:2 NKJV).

Clearly, Noah was well aware which animals God had declared fit for human consumption and which were not suitable for food. This puts one in mind of the time when our Creator used to instruct our ancestors Adam and Eve in the Garden of Eden, as the knowledge of what animals were clean and which were not must have been handed through the generations from Adam down to Noah.

So what then is the connection with the prodigal son having to work with pigs? The link is simply that the pigs are unclean and unclean stands for unholy. The prodigal house of Israel was thrust out of his ancestral land because of his unclean and unholy behavior having forsaken the Law of Moses and rebelled against His Father, the Holy One of Israel. This also seems to sum up the condition of the Church at large which teaches that God's Law has been done away with and that Jesus has nailed it to the cross. If this were true then it would have been an act of gross insubordination, as Jesus has no authority to change the Law of His Father, and He most certainly never would. One can deduce this from the following foundational passage:

"In the beginning was the Word [Torah], and the Word was with God, and the Word was God. And the Word [Torah] became flesh and dwelt [tabernacled] among us, and we beheld His glory, the glory as of the only begotten of the Father, full of grace and truth" (John 1:1&7 NKJV).

Yeshua is the Word [Torah] made flesh! Anyone who says that any portion of the Torah (the Word) is *"done away with"* is saying that Yeshua is done away with. The truth is that our Savior was most emphatic about His respect for His Fathers Law, as He said:

"Do not think I came to destroy the Law or the Prophets. I did not come to destroy but to fulfill" (Matthew 5:17 NKJV).

Fulfill here does not mean cancel, rather it means that He has come to bring the Law/Torah of His Father to its fullest expression. His purpose was to bring it to its completion, by making it possible for us to obey the 'spirit of the Law' through the gift of the Holy Spirit. Yeshua came to magnify the law as He demonstrates in His Sermon on the Mount, where He shows His disciples that sin starts in the mind. This means that even if I think anger, I have already killed my brother; if I even think lust; I have already committed adultery, so that no man can stand justified before the Father by the works of the law alone. This is how He fulfilled the Law of His Father. Furthermore, we need to also take into account that the Spirit of God will never contradict the written word of God, or indeed the word of Yeshua, our Messiah and Redeemer, or else it is a different spirit.

The prodigal son made a life choice, and much like the famous song immortalized by Frank Sinatra; *"I did it My way,"* he walked in disobedience to His Father. He was not prepared to live by God's standards which, had he done so, would have brought him countless blessings. When a man goes against God's standards of righteousness he is likened to a man walking in the face of a mighty wind. But when one repents, he changes direction and goes with the wind that was at one time against him. The Holy One of Israel does not change, His standards of righteousness, His Torah endures forever. Where we stand in relation to it will determine what happens to us. The Prodigal Son rejected the holy for the unholy and the clean for the unclean, and this is why he came to endure the mighty famine, which brings us full circle back to why he ended up with the pigs.

What about the mighty famine, what does it mean?

What about the mighty famine that arose in the land of his exile? Remember, it was the mighty famine which brought the Prodigal Son finally to his senses. Until it happened he seemed oblivious to his true condition. It took the famine to make him aware of this. The famine that Yeshua speaks of in His parable is an allegorical reference to the period the Bible speaks of as the *"time of Jacob's trouble"*, which is designed to bring the Lost House of Israel, i.e. the Prodigal Son to repentance. The *'Time of Jacob's Trouble'* is a time of unprecedented calamity which is prophesied to befall all the 12 tribal sons of Jacob including Judah. It is the same time that Yeshua describes as the *'Great Tribulation'* as recorded in Matthew 24, Mark 13 and Luke 21.

The prophet Jeremiah speaks most eloquently about this time at the end of the age:

'For behold, the days are coming, 'says the LORD, 'that I will bring back from captivity My people Israel and Judah,' says the LORD. 'And I will cause them to return to the land that I gave to their fathers, and they shall possess it.'" Now these are the words that the LORD spoke concerning Israel and Judah.
(Jeremiah 30:3-4 NKJV).

Notice that Jeremiah is addressing his prophecy to the two distinct sons of the Father, i.e. Israel and Judah! The promise is that the eternal God of Israel is going to bring them both back from captivity. We know that God the Father has already started this process, as around 40% of Judah has already returned to the land ever since the establishment of the State of Israel in 1948. It took a holocaust to bring most of them back to the land and the prophecy indicates that it will take another much greater holocaust, this time not for the Jews alone, but for all the Israelite sons of Jacob. The irony is that most of them are not even aware of their Israelite ancestry. The time will come; perhaps we are even now on the threshold of that time, when the whole world will know who and where those missing Israelites are. Jeremiah predicts that their journey back to the land of their fathers is a time of great calamity and tribulation:

"For thus says the LORD:
'We have heard a voice of trembling, of fear, and not of peace. Ask now, and see, whether a man is even in labor with child; So why do I see every man with his hands on his loins like a woman in labor, and all faces pale? Alas! For that day is great, So that none is like it; And it is the time of Jacob's trouble; but he shall be saved out of it. 'For it shall come to pass in that day,' says the LORD of hosts, 'That I will break the yoke from your neck, And will burst your bonds; foreigners shall no more enslave them. But they shall serve the LORD their God, and David their king, whom I will raise up for them." (Jeremiah 30:5-8 NKJV).

Just as the great famine motivated the prodigal son to re-examine his life and situation, so it will also be when the *'Time of Jacob's Trouble'* hits home to those of the Lost House of Israel. Just as the prodigal son lost his prosperity and became totally destitute, so are the people who comprise the ten tribes of Israel destined to suffer the same fate. At the end of the day, their only hope of survival will be to return to the Father's house, i.e. the Land of Israel. They will be a greatly chastened band of returnees. Buffeted as they have by the terrors and terrible trials of the *'Great Tribulation,'* their journey will be a journey of learning as well as return. As they set out on their long journey home; hungry, unwashed, unshaven, with their clothes in tatters, and smelling of pigs, which represents their unclean and unholy lifestyle, they too, like the prodigal son, consider that they are no more worthy to be called their father's sons.

Why is the prodigal son given a new robe by his father?

As they approach the Land they too will discover that their Father has been looking out for them all the time, as He sees them coming from a great way off He will run to greet them with hugs and kisses all-round, this despite their filthy state and the overwhelming smell of pigs which hangs all over them. They will come in a great throng weeping, ready to confess their sins with their eyes full of tears of repentance having come through the manifold tribulations of the 'Time of Jacob's Trouble'. The Prophet Jeremiah puts it very well:

Thus says the LORD: "Refrain your voice from weeping, and your eyes from tears; For your work shall be rewarded, says the LORD, and they shall come back from the land of the enemy. There is hope in your future, says the LORD, That your children shall come back to their own border." (Jeremiah 31:16-17 NKJV).

Israel/Ephraim then confesses how he feels greatly humbled and ashamed. He can literally kick himself for what he has done, and the Prophet Jeremiah movingly records Ephraim's sentiment in the next passage:

"I have surely heard Ephraim (the House of Israel) *bemoaning himself; 'You have chastised me, and I was chastised, like an untrained bull; Restore me, and I will return, For You are the LORD my God. Surely, after my turning, I repented; And after I was instructed, I struck myself on the thigh; I was ashamed, yes, even humiliated, Because I bore the reproach of my youth.'"* (Jeremiah 31:18-19 NKJV).

Notice, it was after they were 'instructed,' that they struck themselves on the thigh and became utterly ashamed. The Hebrew word 'Torah' is generally translated as Law in most English translations, yet the true meaning of Torah is 'instruction'! The Torah is God's instruction in righteousness; it is the teaching that reflects God's own standards. After Ephraim's return, he is going to be instructed all over again, as he needs to undergo a process of re-education. As he discovers more and more what God's standards really are, he will become terribly ashamed of his former lifestyle, and he strikes himself on the thigh. He literally wants to kick himself for not having lived that way, and consequently having missed out on all the blessings that would have flowed from his obedience to the Torah, the instructions of His Father in Heaven.

So what of the robe? Well, it is at this point the Father orders His servants to bring forth the Best Robe, and put it on him. The Robe means that the Prodigal Son from here on is going to be clothed in the Torah – the Living Word. The Robe is in fact the Tallit, (the Jewish prayer shawl), which together with its four fringes (tzit-zis), symbolizes all 613 commandments of the Torah. It is the same robe the Prophet Isaiah speaks of:

""I will greatly rejoice in the LORD, My soul shall be joyful in my God; For He has clothed me with the garments of salvation, He has covered me with the robe of righteousness. As a bridegroom decks himself with ornaments, and as a bride adorns herself with her jewels." (Isaiah 61:10 NKJV).

Being clothed with *the garments of salvation* is to be clothed with the garments of Yeshua, whose Hebrew name signifies salvation. Filled with joy at the return of Ephraim *(the Lost House of Israel)* the Father clothes His long lost children in Yeshua's *Robe of Righteousness.* The Father is filled with joy because now the process of reconciliation between the two estranged houses of Israel, which have been apart for three thousand years, can finally begin.

Why does the father place a ring on the prodigal's hand?

Yes, indeed what of the ring? Why does the Father command His servants to put a ring on his hand? The ring is symbolically very important, as it signifies authority. It was a sign of his high position in the family. The ring is a crested signet ring, representative of the Father's own authority. By placing this ring on the prodigal's hand the Father is acknowledging Ephraim as His firstborn son. The Prophet Jeremiah once again provides confirmation for this:

"For I am a Father to Israel, and Ephraim is MY firstborn" (Jeremiah 31:9b NKJV).

King David also refers to Ephraim's exalted position in the Father's house:

"Ephraim also is the helmet for My head; Judah is My lawgiver"
(Psalms 60:7b NKJV).

Ephraim's helmet is also referred to by the Apostle Paul, as he urges the true disciples of Yeshua to put on the whole armor of God:

"And take the helmet of salvation, and the sword of the Spirit, which is the word of God;" (Ephesians 6:17 NKJV).

Jeremiah gives a further moving passage in which the Father expresses His heart's concern about Ephraim:

"Is Ephraim My dear son? Is he a pleasant child? For though I spoke against him, [in the Time of Jacob's Trouble] I earnestly remember him still; Therefore My heart yearns for him: I will surely have mercy on him, says the LORD"
(Jeremiah 31:20 NKJV).

The Scriptures also provide a precedent for the signet ring of authority being given to Ephraim, as Ephraim is the descendant of Joseph to whom was given the blessing of the birthright by his father the Patriarch Jacob, whose name was changed to Israel. Ephraim upon Jacob's death, according to the right of the 'firstborn' inherited his father's signet ring of authority. (See: Gen 48:11-20 & Gen. 49:22-26). The Bible gives us a further account of Joseph's destiny as a ruler, as he receives his seal of authority from the Pharaoh of Egypt:

And Pharaoh said to Joseph, "See, I have set you over all the land of Egypt." Then Pharaoh took his signet ring of his hand; and put it on Joseph's hand; and he clothed him in garments of fine linen and put a gold chain around his neck. (Genesis 41:41-42 NKJV).

What is the significance of the sandals placed on his feet?

So, what of the sandals? The sandals showed that he was a son instead of a slave, since slaves did not usually wear sandals. They went about barefoot. Yet the sandals serve a much greater purpose than this, as is made clear by the Apostle Paul:

"Having shod your feet with the preparation of the gospel of peace;"
(Ephesians 6:15).

This gospel of peace is none other than the Gospel of the Kingdom which Yeshua and His apostles preached. It is only when our King Messiah, the King of Peace, rules over the restored and reunited kingdom of Israel that the world will finally come to know the meaning of true peace. The Apostle Paul is reflecting the very heart of Our Father in Heaven as he addresses the early believers in Rome, by saying:

"Brethren, my heart's desire and prayer to God for Israel is that they may be saved. And so all Israel (both Houses) will be saved, as it is written:

> *"The deliverer will come out of Zion,*
> *And He will turn away ungodliness*
> *from Jacob;*
> *For this is My covenant with them,*
> *When I take away their sins."*

(Romans 10:1 & Romans 11:26-27 NKJV).

When the prodigal House of Israel returns to the Land of the Father with their hearts full of repentance, they will have their feet shod with the Gospel of Peace. In their subsequent walk, as they wear Yeshua's Garment of Salvation and His Robe of Righteousness, they cannot but exude a powerful example in the house of their Father (the Land of Israel). The Apostle Paul again sums it up in the most beautiful way:

"And how shall they preach unless they are sent? As it is written:

"How beautiful are the feet of those who preach the gospel of peace, Who bring glad tidings of good things!" (Romans 10:15 NKJV).

Why the fatted calf and the great feast?

Imagine what a celebration there will be, both in heaven and in all the earth, when both the Houses of Judah and Israel become One again, having been separated for 3,000 long years! It will be the mother of all celebrations! Can you imagine what a party that will be when finally Messiah the Son of David rules over the REUNITED KINGDOM OF

ISRAEL? In the Book of Revelation this feast is described as the marriage of the Lamb:

"Let us be glad and rejoice and give Him glory, for the marriage of the Lamb has come, and His wife (The Whole House of Israel) has made herself ready."
(Revelation 19:7 NKJV).

Why is the older brother angry?

Why was Judah angry when his younger brother returns to the Father's house? Remember, how in the parable the older brother was angry and would not go in to the party to welcome his long lost brother! Why was he angry? What was his beef? Well, to begin with he did not think his brother deserved to have a great feast, as he made his feelings quite clear to his father, who had come out and pleaded with him to join in the celebrations:

"So he answered and said to his father, 'Lo, these many years I have been serving you; I never transgressed your commandment at any time; and yet you never gave me a young goat, that I might make merry with my friends. 'But as soon as this son of yours came, who has devoured your livelihood with harlots, you killed the fatted calf for him.'
(Luke 15:29-30)

What lies behind Judah's attitude? Why is he not pleased to see his long lost brother return to his father's house? Judah thought that his father was being unfair to him, but he also thought his father was being unjust. He reminded his father that, whilst he had always been an obedient and faithful son, he had never thrown a special party for him and his friends. He also pointed out that his prodigal brother hardly deserved this special treatment in that he had wasted his father's inheritance in cavorting with harlots. He really was quite upset and would not go into the house to meet his brother; he simply could not bring himself to do it. He did not even want to meet his brother. In any case, if the truth be told; he had probably got quite used to being his father's only son.

Actually, Judah's attitude was anticipated by the Prophet Ezekiel. The Tanach (O.T.) prophesied that this kind of reaction would occur. Ezekiel prophesied that in the end times Judah would fear the return of her wayward brothers to the point where they will not want to receive them:

"Son of man, your brethren, your relatives, your countrymen, and all the house of Israel in its entirety, are those about whom the inhabitants of Jerusalem have said, 'Get far away from the LORD; this land has been given to us as a possession.'" V17 Therefore say, "Thus says the LORD GOD: "I will gather you from the peoples, assemble you from the countries where you have been scattered, and I will give you the land of Israel." V19-20 "Then I will give them one heart, and I will put a new spirit within them, and take the stony heart out of their flesh, and give them a heart of flesh, that they may walk in My statutes and keep My judgments and do them, and they shall be My people, and I will be their God." (Ezekiel 11: 15,17,19-20).

The rabbinic leaders of Judah are petrified at the prospect of millions of returning Christian Zionist and Messianic believers from the ten tribes. Can we not understand their fears? They are afraid the Jewish society is going to be swamped by Christians with an evangelizing zeal to make converts of Jews. They are also most afraid of assimilation, as their sons and daughters are swept away in marriage to the newcomers. Notice, the prophecy is that they will be given the land of Israel. Note that it does not mention the fact that they will be given the land of Judah. In other words those returning Israelites will be given the former territory of the Northern Kingdom of Israel to dwell in. This fact alone should make Judah feel somewhat better about the return of his long lost brothers.

Did the older son in the parable have a case?

Humanly speaking the older son most certainly had a reason for being somewhat put out. After all, he was the one who had remained loyal to his father and served him all those years. The fact is that the Jewish people alone (unlike their Israelite brethren of the Lost House of Israel) have borne the mantle of being God's *'chosen'* people, and consequently they have suffered much persecution. Throughout the history of the world the Jews have been the most abused and kicked-around race of people on the earth. The truth is that the world hates the *'Spiritual Realm of God'*, and this is why the world also hates the Jews. Man cannot stand the concept that the Jews are the *'chosen'* people of God.

The Israelites were chosen because they were the 'least' of all people. Thus they were not chosen because they were special; rather they have become special because they were chosen. That God should make a covenant with *'one'* people in itself is an affront to man. A popular Jewish saying goes: *"So, who asked to be chosen?"* It is true they did not ask to be chosen, yet the Jewish people simply know from their four thousand years of experience that they are God's *'chosen'* people. The Jewish cynic will say: *"I wish God had chosen somebody else because it has brought us nothing but pain"*. Whereas it cannot be denied that it has brought them a lot of grief, it has also given them many blessings and it is an awesome privilege and exceptional honour to be *'chosen'* of God. A most important point to remember here is that the Jews were not the only ones who were *'chosen'* by God by a special covenant. We must not forget that the ten tribes of Israel

– those missing sons of Abraham - were also part of that same covenant even though they, unlike the Jews, failed to keep it.

The sole 'SIGN' that identifies

Sadly, the Israelite nations are not aware of their true ancestry as the Lost House of Israel. They do not know who they are. They have forgotten their origins and they think of themselves as Gentiles when in truth they are Israelites. They are ignorant of the fact and so is the rest of the world. The reason they have lost the knowledge of their ancient roots is because they departed from the God of Israel and, especially, because THEY LOST THE ONE "SIGN" THAT WOULD HAVE IDENTIFIED THEM! This sign is mentioned in the Book of Exodus 31:12-13 & 17. . . .

"And the Lord spoke to Moses, saying, "Speak also to the children of Israel, saying: 'Surely My Sabbaths you shall keep, for it is a SIGN between Me and you throughout your generations, that you may know that I am the LORD who sanctifies you . . . . It is a SIGN between Me and the children of Israel forever; for in six days the LORD made the heavens and the earth, and on the seventh day he rested and was refreshed.'"

Here we have the reason that the Israelite nations have lost the knowledge of who they are. They failed to keep God's seventh day Sabbaths, which was the One and Only Sign that would have identified them as God's chosen covenant people. At the same time the Jewish people have never lost their identity as God's chosen people because, ever since they came out of their Babylonian captivity, they have been faithful to God's Sabbaths. Their Sabbath has become known in the world at large as 'the Jewish Sabbath'. It is God's seventh day Sabbath that has more than anything else identified the Jews as 'God's chosen people' and as 'the people of the Covenant'. Being identified to the whole world by the sign of the Sabbath has come at a terrible price for the Jews. We can fairly say that, comparatively speaking, the members of the House of Israel had it easy compared to their brothers of the House of Judah, who being identified as God's chosen people have had it very hard indeed. The other tribes of Israel should have great respect for Judah, as despite continual persecution, rejection and hardship, they have held to their *Torah*, that is to say the *'teaching and instruction'* of their God, regardless of all the suffering it has brought them.

What more can we learn about the older son?

Although a number of Ephraimite believers in Messiah Yeshua have already settled in the Land of Israel, they are forced to live by faith, as the Jewish authorities in the State of Israel will generally only grant them three month visas. Most of them, believing it is the Father's will they remain in the land, will leave briefly, only to re-enter the land on a fresh three monthly visa. Currently the *"Right of Return"* only applies to those who can prove their Jewish origins, and those Ephraimites of the Lost House of Israel at the time of writing have no such right. This explains the reason why the other brother in the parable was not in any way looking out for his lost brother, as he was busy working in the field. Judah today is also not looking for his missing Israelite brothers. In fact most Jews are completely unaware of their existence let alone their whereabouts. It must be said that among the Orthodox community there are numerous rabbis and Torah scholars who are familiar with the words of the Prophets about the ultimate return of the Ten Tribes, and the promises of the Restoration of the United Kingdom of Israel. Ironically, the Sidur, the Jewish prayer book, contains the Amidah prayer in which the observant Jews pray three times a day for the return of their lost brothers from the house of Israel. It forms an intrinsic part of the Messianic Hope of Israel, yet even so, most Jews are utterly unaware of the identity or the whereabouts of their Israelite brothers today. Some few are even now working for the ultimate reconciliation and restoration of the two houses of Israel. However, for the vast majority of the Jewish nation the question does not even arise, as their main concern is a mixture of simply making a decent living for themselves and their families, and plain survival in this competitive and increasingly uncertain and dangerous world of ours. They are not looking for their brother's return, and thus the way the parable describes Judah's attitude fits the present situation well.

What did the father mean by saying; "Your brother was dead and is alive again?"

We know that in reality the prodigal son was not dead, as he had to be alive to survive the famine and arrive at his father's house. So, what did the father mean by saying to Judah, his older son; your brother was dead? As always we find that the Bible interprets itself, and we find the answer in God's instruction to Moses regarding the way to treat a wayward and rebellious son:

"If a man has a stubborn and rebellious son who will not obey the voice of his father or the voice of his mother, and who, when they have chastened him, will not heed them, "then his father and his mother shall take hold of him and bring him out to the elders of his city, to the gate of his city. "And they shall say to the elders of his city, 'This son of ours is stubborn and rebellious; he will not obey our voice; he is a glutton and a drunkard.' Then all the men of his city shall stone him to death with stones; so you shall put away the evil from among you, and all Israel shall hear

and fear. "If a man has committed a sin deserving of death, and he is put to death, and you hang him on a tree, his body shall not remain overnight on the tree, but you shall surely bury him that day, so that you do not defile the land which the LORD your God is giving you as an inheritance; for he who is hanged is accursed of God.'" (Deuteronomy 21:18-23 NKJV).

The prodigal son rebelled against his father's house, as he took his inheritance and wasted it with *'riotous'* living, according to the KJV. The Hebrew word for *'riotous'* is *'zalal,'* which also means *'glutton', 'drunkard', and 'waster'.* Gesenius' Hebrew- Chaldee Lexicon interprets it as follows: *"one who squanders his own body."* Even the letters of *'zalal'* give us a further fascinating insight in the deep meaning of this word. All the letters of the Hebrew alphabet have not only an individual meaning, but they also each have their own numerical value and these values in turn have meaning also. Thus even the letters and the numbers convey a picture of what lies beneath the surface of the text. *"Zalal"* is spelled *"zayin-lamed-lamed".* The letter *'zayin'* is the *'sword'* or *'to cut off'.* Lamed is *'the shepherd's staff'* and *'learning'* or *'teaching'.* The full meaning therefore is that this rebellious son has *"cut himself off from the Shepherds staff and all that he has been taught".* The rebellious son in this parable is of course none other than Ephraim representing the Lost House of Israel. Moses speaks of the Ten Tribes of Israel in the same terms, those of a rebellious son. This means that according to the Torah, Ephraim has earned the penalty of the rebellious son. This punishment was to be "death" and the body was to be hung on a tree.

The good news is that, as in the example of the parable, God the Father never gave up on that son. Our Abba saw us while we were yet far off; while we were trying to find our way home, and He had compassion on us. He sent His own Son in the flesh to die the death of the rebellious son. He was hung on a tree and yet taken down before sundown and buried that same day, exactly as Torah prescribes. That is why the father in the parable was able to exclaim to his other son Judah:

"Son, you are always with me, and all that I have is yours. It was right that we should make merry and be glad, for your brother was dead and is alive again, and was lost and is found!"

CHAPTER FOUR

THE PARABLE OF THE WIZE AND FOOLISH VIRGINS

ᘒ\ᘓ

The Parables contain a Hidden Message and a Mystery!

One of the most remarkable and frequently overlooked facts about the parables is the revelation that Yeshua spoke in parables in order to hide the truth. As we have already seen in the previous chapter, it is not generally understood that the reason our Messiah spoke in parables was because the message He really wanted to convey was not intended for general consumption. Once we truly understand this aspect we will never look at any of His parables in the same light again.

Having just related the Parable of the Sower to a great multitude gathered on the seashore of Lake Galilee, Yeshua concludes His remarks with: *"He who has ears to hear, let him hear!"* His own disciples had heard every word, yet even they had not understood the meaning:

"But when He was alone, those around Him with the twelve asked Him about the parable. And He said to them, "To you it has been given to know the MYSTERY of the

kingdom of God; but to those outside, all things come in parables, so that…..

'Seeing they may see and not perceive, and hearing they may hear and not understand; lest they should turn, and their sins be forgiven them'"

And He said to them, "Do you not understand this parable? How then will you understand all the parables?" (Mark 4:9-13 NKJV)

Yeshua then went on to teach His chosen disciples (*those who were with the twelve*) the meaning of His parable. For extra emphasise the same account is repeated in Luke 8:9-10, and these Scriptures put a wholly different connotation on how we should look at the parables. The inference is clear in that our perceptions of what a particular parable means may not be correct. Most of us are inclined to look at the surface meaning of the words and draw what we see as the moral message we think Yeshua is trying to convey to His audience. Generally we do not look for some subtext or hidden meaning. Nevertheless, going by Yeshua's own words there is a hidden meaning. The key to understanding the hidden message in any parable lies in Yeshua's words to His disciples when He said to them: *"To you it has been given to know the MYSTERY of the kingdom of God."* The big question is how can we know the mysteries of the kingdom of God?

Part of the answer lies in the very last question the disciples ever asked Yeshua. The setting was 40 days after Yeshua's resurrection and immediately before He left this earth to return to His Father, when the disciples could not contain themselves any longer as they asked Him the question that was burning in their hearts. *"When are you going to restore the Kingdom to Israel?"* In their hearts they assumed that this was what He was going to do all along, but how shocking for them to see all their hopes die when the Romans crucified Him! However, to their utter amazement He rose from the dead three days and three nights after He was put into the grave and their messianic hopes for the restoration of the kingdom to Israel soared once again. Previous to this moment the disciples had come to Yeshua privately and asked Him eagerly: *What will be the sign of your coming and the end of the age?* (Matthew 24:3) Yeshua then proceeded to unveil what has become known as the "Olivet Prophecy" in which He listed all the events that would take place leading up to His coming. That was the reason for the question: *"Lord will you at this time restore the kingdom to Israel?"* (Acts 1:6 NKJV)

When Yeshua had finished listing all the signs that would precede His Second coming, He told His disciples not to fall into the destructive traps of apathy, unbelief, faithlessness, and inaction. He then emphasised these same points over and over again in seven parables: The fig tree (Matthew 24:32-35), the days of Noah (24:36-41), the thief (24:42-44), the unfaithful steward (24:45-51), the ten virgins (25: 1-13), the talents (25: 14-30), and the sheep and the goats (25:31-51). Notice that the whole context and focus of the Olivet Prophecy and the seven subsequent parables of exhortation is the establishment of the kingdom to Israel.

In one way or another, the theme of each one of these parables highlights the differences between disciples of Yeshua, who have an understanding of the times and who act accordingly, and those who do not have an understanding of the times and who are therefore ill-equipped to act. It is in this context that Yeshua related the Parable of the Ten Virgins.

The Parable of the Ten Virgins

READ: Matthew 25:1-13

"Then the kingdom of heaven shall be likened to ten virgins who took their lamps and went out to meet the bridegroom."

Why did Yeshua begin this parable with the word, *"Then?"* He wanted His followers to understand that the parable was for the future. It was designed to especially emphasise that the message of the parable was for the time known as the end of the age, when all the signs He had listed in Matthew 24 had come to pass.

A most interesting question is: Who do the *"ten virgins"* represent? Prophetically speaking, when we read about the number ten as referring to people, we should consider the possibility that it might refer to the wayward and scattered house of Israel, which is comprised of ten tribes. The context of the parable also appears to confirm this as the over-riding subject of the whole discourse is the restoration of the kingdom to Israel. Another interesting example of this association with the number ten can be found in the Book of Zechariah, where the prophet uses the number ten in a symbolic fashion to refer to the lost house of Israel:

"Thus saith the LORD of hosts; In those days it shall come to pass, that ten men shall take hold out of all languages of the nations, even shall take hold of the skirt of him that is a Jew, saying, We will go with you: for we have heard that God is with you.'" (Zechariah 8:23 KJV)

The reference to the skirts of the Jew here indicates the ten tribes getting hold of the tzit-zits (tassels) fixed onto the four corners of the Jewish prayer shawl, which symbolise the 613 instructions of the Torah. How on earth can this

71

be? Does it make sense that God would refer to the House of Israel as "virgins" when they were cast out of the land for rebellion and idolatry, i.e. a type of spiritual adultery? Well, it is not as extraordinary as it appears at first sight, as Jeremiah the Prophet, speaking in the same context of the restoration of the house of Israel to the Land of Israel, makes exactly the same reference:

"At the same time, says the Lord, "I will be the God of all the families of Israel, and they shall be My people." Thus says the LORD: "The people who survived the sword found grace in the wilderness – Israel, when I went to give him rest." The LORD has appeared of old to me, saying: "Yes, I have loved you with an everlasting love; therefore with loving kindness have I drawn you. Again I will build you, and you shall be rebuilt, O VIRGIN OF ISRAEL!" (Jeremiah 31:1-4 NKJV)

In this most remarkable prophecy Jeremiah gives us three revelations:

FIRST: God promises that He will be the Elohim of 'ALL' the families of Israel, i.e. not just the Jewish members of the family.

SECOND: Realising that Israel has sinned against Him, He still refers to Israel as a "virgin." Why? Simply because He is the potter and we are the clay and, as a potter looking at the unsightly lump of clay before him, our Father already envisages the finished article He is going to create.

THIRD: He promises to restore them to their former homes in Samaria, the capital of the northern kingdom of Israel (See verse 5). *"You shall yet plant vines on the mountains of Samaria."*

The Book of Revelation provides yet further confirmation, as in referring to: *"A Lamb standing on Mount Zion, and with Him one hundred and forty four thousand,*** having His Father's name written on their foreheads."* This sets the scene for the return of Messiah Yeshua, the Lamb of Elohim. It then goes on to say: *"These are the ones who were not defiled with women, for they are VIRGINS. These are the ones who follow the Lamb wherever He goes. These were redeemed from among men, being first fruits to God and to the Lamb.* (Revelation 14:1 & 4-5 NKJV)

We can reasonably deduce from the above examples that the Bible uses the term *"virgin"* to label those of us who are in the process of returning to God (Elohim) and to our Hebrew roots from among the lost house of Israel. Clearly, this interpretation has far-reaching implications about the meaning of the parable of the ten virgins, as it focuses on non-Jewish disciples. It is a parable about a specific message for Ephraim. It is for those of Jesus Christ's (Yeshua's) disciples who wish to return to their Father's House and who being aware of the times are actively preparing themselves for His second coming. *****Revelation 7:3-8 clearly indicates that these 144,000 are from the twelve tribes of Israel, including the so-called 'lost' tribes of Israel.**

The Lamps – What does it mean?

What is the meaning of the lamps in this parable? What did Yeshua mean by saying that the ten virgins 'took their lamps?' We find part of the answer in the following Scriptures:

"For the commandment is a lamp, and the Law (Torah) a light." (Proverbs 6:23)

"Your word is a lamp to my feet and a light to my path."
(Psalms 119:105)

Many scholars have correctly seen the connection between the lamps in the parable and the Law/Torah nevertheless; it alone cannot explain the full meaning of the parable. The reason for this is that the lamps belonging to some of the virgins went out! (Matthew 25:8) Clearly, the Torah, the eternal Word of God, does not go out! Rather what goes out is the light of the Torah in an individual disciple. The light of the Torah should be clearly evident in the lives of the followers of Jesus (Yeshua), the Messiah of Israel. This is the meaning of Paul's words to the Galatians:

"I have been crucified with Christ; it is no longer I who live, but Christ lives in me; and the life which I now live in the flesh I live by faith in the Son of God, who loved me and gave Himself for me." (Galatians 2:20 NKJV)

Remember that Yeshua is the Word/Torah made flesh! As Messiah lives in us, our light, i.e. the light of the Torah in us, shines out for all to see so that all may eventually give honour to our Father in heaven for His beautiful gifts. Yeshua explained it like this:

"You are the light of the world. A city that is set on a hill cannot be hidden. Nor do they light a lamp and put it under a basket, but on a lamp stand, and it gives light to all in the house. Let your light so shine before men, that they may see your good works and glorify your Father in heaven." (Matthew 5:14-16 NKJV).

Therefore we can conclude that the "lamp" represents the life of a disciple of Jesus (Yeshua) who lives the Word.

We find further support for this premise in the Book of Proverbs:

"The spirit of a man is the lamp of the LORD, searching all the inner depths of his heart." (Proverbs 20:27 NKJV)
"The light of the righteous rejoices, but the lamp of the wicked will be put out." (Proverbs 13:9 NKJV)

Thus without a doubt, the Scriptures use the symbol of a lamp to indicate how a man conducts his life in the light of the Torah.

Five Wise Virgins and Five Foolish ones

"Now five of them were wise, and five were foolish. Those who were foolish took their lamps and took no oil with them. But the wise took oil in their vessels with their lamps"

We now understand two important facts about this parable: (1) the ten virgins symbolically represent disciples from the ten northern tribes of Israel, i.e. Ephraim, who are returning to God (Elohim) through Jesus (Yeshua) the Messiah, and (2) the lamps represent the light of the Torah in the lives of these disciples.

Can we see further evidence of this symbolism in the fact that five of the virgins were wise and five were foolish? What do the Scriptures have to say about being wise or foolish? Just consider the following verses:

"The wise in heart will receive commandments, but the prating fool shall fall."
(Proverbs 10:8 KJV)

"The law of the LORD is perfect converting the soul: the testimony of the LORD is sure, enlightening the eyes." (Psalm 19:7 KJV)

"Whoso keepeth the law is a wise son: but he that is a companion of riotous men shameth his father." (Proverbs 28:7 KJV)

These and many other verses in the Bible affirm the fact that a wise man is someone who clings to the instructions of Torah and performs it, while a foolish man is someone who forsakes the Torah or ignores it altogether.

We have even more support for our premise when we consider the significance of the number five in Hebrew thought. So, what is the significance of number five? The number five is symbolic of the Torah itself. How is that? The foundation of all Scripture is the five books of Moses, the first five books of the Bible. When Jesus (Yeshua) said five of them were foolish and five were wise, He was explaining the sole criterion which would determine whether a virgin was wise or foolish, i.e. it was her response to His Torah which would decide the issue.

What is the meaning of the Oil in the Vessel?-

What is the oil that the wise virgins took in their vessels? And what are the vessels the oil went into? The vessels represent the mind or heart of the disciple while the oil represents the anointing of the Holy Spirit of Elohim (the setapart spirit of God). Notice what happened to David when Samuel anointed him:

"Then Samuel took the horn of oil, and anointed him in the midst of his brethren: and the Spirit of the LORD came upon David from that day forward..." (Samuel 16:13 KJV)

The anointing oil is symbolic of the outpouring of the Holy Spirit (Hebrew = Ruach haKodesh). This explains why the anointing takes place on the head. Even as oil is literally poured on the head, the request is made that the LORD (YHVH) pour His Spirit into the mind of the one anointed. David understood this clearly for he wrote:

"Thou preparest a table before me in the presence of mine enemies: thou anointest my head with oil; my cup runneth over." (Psalm 23:5 KJV)

Thus, as sheep under the care of the Good Shepherd, we ought to ask for the set-apart anointing on our head so that our minds might be filled with the knowledge of Elohim. Since this anointing takes place on our heads, i.e. in our minds, the anointing primarily involves our intellect. It involves what we do with our minds and whether or not we are filling them with the word of God (Elohim). This involves the study and the application (the doing) of Torah in our lives. It directly relates to whether or not we are responding to the *SHEMA*, *the* greatest commandment in the Torah.

"Hear (Shema), O Israel: the LORD our God, the LORD is one! You shall love the Lord your God with all your heart, with all your soul, and with all your strength. And these words which I command you today shall be in your heart. You shall teach them diligently to your children, and shall talk of them when you sit in your house, when you walk by the way, when you lie down, and when you rise up." (Deuteronomy 6:47 NKJV)

This clearly takes much effort. So, how do we ensure that "these words" end up in our heart? The answer is simple; we have to put them there! It does not happen automatically, but only as we exert a concerted effort to place them there. King David, the great psalmist of Israel wrote about this very thing:

"With my whole heart I have sought you; oh, let me not wander from Your commandments! Your word I have hidden in my heart, that I might not sin against You." (Psalm 119:11 NKJV)

Now this is a beautiful prelude to the New (*renewed*) Covenant which the LORD (YHVH) promises to make with all the families of Israel.

"Behold, the days are coming, says the LORD, when I will make a new covenant with the house of Israel, and with the house of Judah – not according to the covenant [B'rit] that I made with their fathers in the day that I took them by the hand to lead them out of the land of Egypt, My covenant [B'rit] which they broke, though I was a husband to them, says the LORD. "But this is the covenant [B'rit] that I will make with the house of Israel after those days, says the LORD: I will put My law [Torah] in their minds, and write it on their hearts; and I will be their God, and they shall be My people. (Jeremiah 31:31-33 NKJV)

As David wrote: *"I delight to do Your will, O my God, and Your law [Torah] is within my heart."* (Psalm 40:8 NKJV) When we study the Word of God and live by its precepts, it is as if our lives become oil lamps and the wicks of our minds soak up the oil of the Spirit. The human brain acts naturally much like a sponge as it soaks up fresh information. Symbolically our brain is the wick of our oil lamp which needs to continuously draw up the oil by drinking in the Word. The more our mind becomes saturated with the Word of God (Elohim), the more our lamps will be filled with oil. In doing what the Torah commands, as we begin to live by God's own standards, the light of the Torah within us shines forth as light in the world peeling back the darkness all around us. The Apostle Peter puts it in another way: *"And we are His witnesses to these things, and so is also the Holy Spirit whom God has given to those who obey Him"* (Acts 5:32)

Notice, how Peter emphasises the word obey! It must be said that obedience does not come naturally to mankind, as ever since the Garden of Eden man's natural instinct has been to rebel and go his own way. Nevertheless, it is the absolute requirement to receiving the anointing of YHVH's set-apart Spirit, the Spirit of Truth. Yeshua, our Messiah, spoke most emphatically on this same issue:

"If you love Me, keep My commandments. And I will pray the Father, and He will give you another Helper, that He may abide with you forever – "the Spirit of truth, whom the world cannot receive, because it neither sees Him nor knows Him, but you know Him, for He dwells with you and will be in you." (John 14:15-17 NKJV)

Notice, Yeshua's statement starts with *"If"* you love Me. By saying; *'IF' you love Me, keep My commandments,* He is in effect asking us to prove our love for Him. He is asking us to put our money where our mouth is so to speak. He is telling us that the only way we can prove our love for Him is in keeping His commandments, and He then goes on to say that He will send us another Helper, the Spirit of Truth. The clear inference here is that there are conditions attached to receiving the Holy Spirit. Yeshua then goes on to say:

"He who has My commandments and keeps them, it is he who loves Me. And he who loves Me will be loved by My Father, and I will love Him and manifest Myself to Him." (John 14:21 NKJV)

Notice, that it is the keeping of His commandments that is the key to demonstrating our love for Him, and it is also the key to receiving both His love and the love of the Father. Once this vital condition of keeping His commandments has been met, He promises to *"manifest"* Himself to us. How does He manifest Himself? He does it through the *Comforter* or *Helper,* the Spirit of Truth.

For those who believe that the commandments are done away with, or that the commandments of Jesus (Yeshua), our Saviour and Redeemer, are any different from those of His Father, we need only look at Yeshua's own words on this matter.

"If you keep My commandments, you will abide in My love, just as I have kept My Father's commandments and abide in His love." (John 15:10 NKJV)

The point about the oil in our lamps shining forth the light is determined by the extent to which we demonstrate our love for Elohim through our obedience to His command-ments.Yeshua (Jesus) said:

"Do not lay up for yourselves treasures on earth, where moth and rust destroy and where thieves break in and steal; but lay up for yourselves treasures in heaven, where nei-ther moth nor rust destroys and where thieves do not break in and steal. "For where your treasure is there your heart will be also. The lamp of the body is the eye. If therefore your eye is good, your whole body will be full of light. "But if your eye is bad, your whole body will be full of darkness. If therefore the light that is in you is darkness, how great is that darkness! "No one can serve two masters; for either he will hate the one and love the other, or else he will be loyal to one and despise the other. You cannot serve God and mammon." (Mathew 6:19-24 NKJV)

Do you know what the treasure is that Jesus Christ (Messiah Yeshua) wants us to *"Lay up"* for ourselves? It is the Torah, *"the Word"* of God (Elohim). In fact He is actually borrowing this beautiful metaphor from the Torah:

"Therefore you shall 'lay up' these 'words' of mine in your heart and in your soul, and bind them as a sign on your hand, and they shall be as frontlets between your eyes." (Deuteronomy 11:18 NKJV)

If we store up the Word of God (Elohim) into our minds, and actually walk in obedience to that word in our lives, then we show by our commitment that we have a generous spirit. This is what Yeshua meant by saying that *"the light of the body is in the eye,"* the eye being used as a metaphor which speaks of our spirit, whether generous or stingy. How much oil gets drawn up the wick of our minds, and therefore, how much light is given off, inversely depends on how much we love material wealth or mammon. If we love it, and the, *"love of money is the root of all evil"* (1 Timothy 1:6), then we have *"an evil eye,"* which is a Hebraic expression for being stingy or cheap. On the other hand, if we value material wealth only to the extent that we can use it to serve God (Elohim) and love our neighbour, then we have a generous or bountiful eye.

"He who has a generous eye will be blessed, for he gives his bread to the poor." (Proverbs 22:9 NKJV)

The apostle Paul considered it necessary to exhort the Thessalonians not to *"quench the Spirit"* (1Thessalonians 5:19). This is the meaning of Yeshua's words about the foolish virgins. They were not pouring the Word of God (Elohim) into their minds through the Spirit of Truth, and they were not soaking up its meaning unto obedient and faithful living. That is why when the midnight cry of the bridegroom came they found themselves without oil for their lamps.

While the Bridegroom Tarried

"While the bridegroom was delayed, they all slumbered and slept."

We need to be careful not to take this statement out of context. Here, slumbering and sleeping is not necessarily symbolic of spiritual laziness, but rather a fact of life. We all need to sleep at night. After all, remember that five of the virgins were wise. Therefore, it is hard to believe that just after Yeshua said that some of the virgins were wise, that He would say that 'all' of them were spiritually asleep. So, what then does this part of the parable mean? It simply means that the midnight call comes not only at an unexpected time of the day, but at the worst possible part of the day, in the dead of night. How inconvenient is that!

However, that is the point. The foolish reconed that they would have plenty of time in the morning to get oil for their lamps, whereas the wise understood that the midnight call could come at an 'awkward' time and that they might need oil at all times. After all, who would need to walk around in the middle of the night? Hundreds of nights had already passed without the call. Maybe the foolish virgins became exasperated by what seemed like an interminable wait and they allowed things to slip. The wise on the other hand kept vigilant night after night regardless of the circumstances. At a time which turned out to be unexpected and inconvenient, the wise were ready.

The Midnight Cry!

So, what is the meaning of the midnight cry? What does midnight symbolise, and what is the cry that takes place at that time? The darkness of night symbolises the Great Tribulation also known as the time of Jacob's Trouble. It is at this prophetic time that that the call goes out to meet the bridegroom. This is the time prophesied by Yeshua in His Olivet Prophecy:

"For as lightning comes from the east and flashes to the west, so also will the coming of the Son of Man be. "For wherever the carcass is, there the eagles will be gathered together. "Immediately after the tribulation of those days the sun will be darkened, and the moon will not give its light; the stars will fall from heaven, and the powers of the heavens will be shaken. "Then the sign of the Son of Man will appear in heaven, and then all the tribes of the earth will mourn, and they will see the Son of Man coming on the clouds of heaven with power and great glory."
(Matthew 24:27-30 NKJV)

This is also the time mentioned in the parable about the days of Noah:

"But as the days of Noah were, so also will the coming of the Son of Man be. "For as in the days before the flood, they were eating and drinking, marrying and giving in marriage, until the day that Noah entered the ark, and did not know until the flood came and took them all away, so also will the coming of the Son of Man be.

"Then two men will be in the field: one will be taken and the other left. "Two women will be grinding at the mill: one will be taken and the other left. "Watch therefore,

for you do not know what hour your Lord is coming."
(Matthew 24:38-42 NKJV)

Notice, that in this example again we have half of the
people taken and the other half is left behind! What deter-
mines whether one is taken or left behind? Have we not
already explained the answer in relation to the Parable of
the Ten Virgins? Is it not determined by the walk and the life
of the individual, by whether or not the person has demon-
strated his love for Jesus (Yeshua), consistently adhering to
His Torah by keeping His commandments?
Can we see the connection to what the Prophet Jeremiah
had to say to the house of Israel?

"Return, O backsliding children," says the LORD; "for I
am married to you. I will take you, one from a city and two
from a family, and I will bring you to Zion."
(Jeremiah 3:14 NKJV)

This is also the time mentioned in the parable of the thief:

"But know this, that if the master of the house had known
what hour the thief would come, he would have watched
and not allowed his house to be broken into. "Therefore
you also be ready, for the Son of Man is coming at an hour
you do not expect." (Matthew 24:43-44 NKJV)

We could go on to relate the parable of the unfaithful
steward, but the point is that all of these parables have the
same focus, yet they are each told from a different perspective. What is that single focus? It is the return of the ten tribes
to the land of Israel prior to the return of Messiah, as He
comes to establish His Kingdom over the Reunited Kingdom
of Israel. It is at this time when the two faces of Israel will
once again become one in the hand of God (Elohim).

This may not be how you once understood these parables, but please do not reject this interpretation out of hand, and remember that they were written for our admonition, not for some one else's. Yeshua taught them and inspired others to preserve them because He knew that many of us would become overly content with ourselves in the last days.

So, what then is the Midnight Cry? It is the invitation and opportunity presented to Ephraim for his return to the Land of Israel in anticipation of Messiah's coming. Remember, the parable speaks to the ten northern tribes, i.e. the ten virgins of Israel, not to the Jewish disciples. Judah already has the opportunity to live and work in the land, but Ephraim has been barred by Israeli law from partaking of this privilege. Yeshua promised that the invitation to go forth to meet Him as He returns to Jerusalem will go out at the darkest hour of the day, i.e. at midnight.

How easy it would be to rationalise not going out to meet the bridegroom when we hear the midnight cry. After all, the possibility that the regathering of the tribes would take place before Messiah's return is not exactly a mainstream belief, neither is it an attractive one. Would you get up and move to the land of Israel if the opportunity presented itself? Maybe you would consider it safer to wait until after the Messiah comes? Would your decision be based on Scripture or on fear? What if the safest place on earth would be in Israel? Think about it! The calmest place during a hurricane is in the eye of the storm, with all of the chaos swirling all around. What if YHVH, in all of His infinite wisdom and insight, set it up this way in order to separate the tares from the wheat? (Matthew 13:30) What if our Father wants to know who really wants to dwell in and inherit the land He promised to our ancestors? What if our Father wants to see who really trusts Him? What if an apparently "safe" place today turns into an absolute disaster zone right after the wise virgins go out to meet the bridegroom by moving to Israel *before Messiah's* return?

The Wise have no Oil to Give!

"Then all those virgins arose and trimmed their lamps. "And the foolish said to the wise, 'give us some of your oil, for our lamps are going out.' "But the wise answered, saying, 'No, lest there should not be enough for us and you; but go rather to those who sell, and buy for yourselves.'"

How is it that those wise virgins cannot give even just a little of their oil to the foolish ones? Are they not being rather mean? Not at all, for what the foolish ask cannot be given by the wise. The wise cannot give to the foolish because it is not theirs to give. The presence of the oil in the vessels is a daily choice that we each individually need to make; we cannot make it on behalf of someone else. It requires labouring in the Word of Elohim and taking the time to learn and absorb the wisdom so that over time a strong commitment is built up.

As the Proverb relates: *"Buy the truth, and do not sell it, also wisdom and instruction and understanding."* (Proverbs 23:23 NKJV)

Buying and selling are figures of speech highlighting the importance of acquiring these things. We do not obtain them by purchasing them, but rather by decisions we make in our lives. We "Buy" them with our time and effort spent. This is the case with truth, wisdom, instruction, and understanding, just as it is with the oil for the vessels.

However much the wise wanted to help the foolish, they had only one choice to make and that was to leave the foolish virgins to reap the consequences for what they had sown for themselves. Just as it is with a good vintage, we humans cannot become mature overnight, but only over a period of time. In effect, we are actually making our future decisions to respond to the midnight call right now each and every day.

Only those that are ready!

"And while they went to buy, the bridegroom came, and those who were ready went in with him to the wedding; and the door was shut. "Afterward the other virgins came also, saying, 'Lord, Lord, open to us!' "But he answered and said, 'Assuredly, I say to you, I do not know you.' "Watch therefore, for you know neither the day nor the hour in which the Son of Man is coming."

Notice how the virgins address the bridegroom by saying: *"Lord, Lord."* Notice also, how the bridegroom addresses the foolish virgins, as he says: *"I do not know you!"*
Does this not remind you of a previous statement Yeshua made in His Sermon on the Mount?

"Not everyone who says to Me, 'Lord, Lord,' shall enter the kingdom of heaven, but he who does the will of My Father in heaven. "Many will say to Me in that day, 'Lord, Lord, have we not prophesied in Your name, cast out demons in Your name, and done many wonders in Your name?' "And I will declare to them, 'I never knew you; depart from Me, you who practice lawlessness!'" (Matthew 7:21-23 NKJV)

Remember, the parable of the five wise and five foolish virgins, like all the other parables are a particular Hebraic way of teaching in which Yeshua wanted to convey certain principles pertaining to His kingdom. Yeshua invariably is using a metaphor and He never intended them to be taken literally. The point of the parable is to call His disciples from among the lost sheep of the house of Israel to action, for the time will come when action will be required and any delay will result in loss.
The bridegroom in the parable is of course, the Son of Man [the second Adam], a label of humility that Yeshua

(Jesus) used to describe Himself. In the course of the parable, He used the pre-nuptial ceremonies and customs of ancient Israel to illustrate the importance of being watchful and being prepared.

The wise Virgins are to have a Jewish Wedding!

The Jewish wedding customs in the days of Messiah were very different from what they are today in our society. When a young man saw a woman he was particularly interested in, he would not go up to the girl and ask her for her hand in marriage. Oh no, the rules were very different then. He would go to his father and request of his father that a marriage contract be arranged. All becomes clear once you understand the Jewish wedding customs of the time.

The father of the groom would approach the father of the bride. He would have his son with him. They would have a contract and a sum of money with them. – A PRICE FOR THE BRIDE (the Blood of the Lamb)! The Father of the Groom would present the contract to the father of the bride. They would then pour a CUP OF WINE and at that point the girl would be asked to come in, and her father would inform her of the contract and proposal of marriage. She would wear a veil over her face for modesty (I dare say, she would be having a jolly good look at the young man through her veil). Her father would then ask her: *"Will you take this cup?"* She had to decide right there and then! If she picks up the cup and drinks from it, her entire life is changed from that instant. She is betrothed – she is committed – there is no going back – she is no longer available to anyone else – she is spoken for. That's it! The betrothal is not a mere engagement; it takes a bill of divorce to break it. *She drinks some of the wine – she then gives the cup to the young man and he drinks some of the wine and THEY HAVE BECOME BETROTHED.*

It's a Contract between two Fathers

Remember the words of John 18:11, where Yeshua at the time of His arrest in the Garden of Gethsemane says: *"The cup which My Father has given Me shall I not drink it?"* Can you see the connection? This is a type of the Cup of Redemption – the Third Cup of the Passover Service (Hagadah). Marriage is a blood covenant and it is a type of our eventual union with our future Groom Yeshua (Jesus), the Messiah of Israel and Savior of the world. After the two youngsters have drunk from the cup, the two fathers sign the marriage contract; remember, it is a contract between two fathers! One is a type of God the Father in Heaven, who is the father of the Groom, His only begotten Son; whilst the other is a type of your father the Devil, the god of this world. Just before the Groom and his Father are about to leave, the groom walks over to his fiancée and intended bride and says to her:

"I am going to prepare a place for you and when it is ready I will come back to take you to myself" (John 14:2-3 NKJV).

When Yeshua spoke these same words to His disciples they knew exactly what He was talking about. They knew He was talking about a marriage relationship. They knew the words He was saying, just as any Jewish boy would have known them. They did not necessarily understand the spiritual significance of His words at the time, but they knew what He was saying, as those words were taken right out of the Jewish Marriage Custom of that day.

Marriage is the closest possible and most intimate relationship of all relationships known to man, and yet, that is the very relationship God wants to have with us! Yeshua (Jesus) has spoken these words to you also, and He has gone away to prepare a place for you. His plan is to come again to receive you to Himself, so that where He is you can be also. The

House He is preparing for you is His Fathers House, it is a huge estate situated in the Land of Greater Israel, stretching all the way from the River Nile to the River Euphrates, and it has many mansions. One of them maybe for you! It may have your name on it! However, there are conditions, as we have seen in the parable of the virgins, as it depends on whether you chose to be wise or foolish.

Once the Groom has gone the Bride knows she has approximately nine to fifteen months to wait for the bride-groom to return. She never knows the exact date of her wedding! Her future husband has not only to build the house for her, he has also to prepare the place as well. When he has built the place for her – her new home – he has made it as beautiful as he can possibly make it. Yet, even then, he doesn't decide he is ready to fetch his bride. Rather it is his father who decides when he can go to fetch her. So, when he has finished the home, he goes to his father, and asks him to inspect the place to see if everything is the way it should be. Only, when his father gives his permission, can the bride-groom go to get his bride. Do you see the significance of what is being said?

"But of that day and that hour no one knows, not even the angels in heaven, but My Father only." (Matthew 24:36 NKJV)

You see it is the Father who decides when our Divine and heavenly Groom is to come for His bride.

Meanwhile the bride is busily preparing herself for the wedding. She has been making clothes by hand, and is pre-paring her trousau (*studying the Torah)* for her future life with her husband. She has been preparing her cooking skills. Her mother and her sisters have been helping her with the preparations. She is learning all sorts of things of her mother (the Body of Messiah/Church), all the special recipes that will please her husband to be. The Holy Spirit, the Spirit of Truth has been helping her to develop her talents in every way, so that she may become the best possible bride without any spots or wrinkles. (Ephesians 5:27)

Once the nine months have elapsed the bridesmaids come each night to spend the night with the bride in readiness for the call when it comes. *(There could be a possible connection here with the last three and a half years of the Time of Jacob's Trouble e.g. the Great Tribulation).* From now on, the bridegroom could come almost any night. Can you sense the suspense of these ladies? Imagine the sheer excitement in the house of the bride! The air of expectation in the house! Isn't it wonderful? Isn't this romantic? What an adventure it all is! Once the Bridegroom receives permission from His Father, he gathers his friends and they set out late at night. He then sends out his friend ahead of him to arrive at least an hour before him and before he and his party get to the house of the bride.

The end-time ministry of Elijah the prophet

What does the friend of the groom do? Well, the best man gets to the bride's house late at night when its pitch dark and every one is asleep, and he then shouts at the top of his voice' "THE BRIDEGROOM IS COMING!" He thus wakes up the whole neighbourhood. It is 'MIDNIGHT' and in the commotion lights are going on everywhere as he shouts again and again' "THE BRIDEGROOM IS COMING!" (Matthew 25:6).

The role of the best man is symbolic of the ministry of Elijah that is spoken of by the Prophet Malachi:

"Behold I send you Elijah the prophet before the coming of the great and dreadful Day of the Lord." (Malachi 4:5)

The first fulfilment of this was just prior to the First Coming of Messiah Yeshua, when John the Baptist appeared on the scene as: *"The voice of one crying in the wilderness: Prepare the way of the Lord; Make his paths straight." He came into the wilderness saying: "REPENT, FOR THE KINGDOM OF HEAVEN IS AT HAND."* This John the Baptist came in the spirit and the power of Elijah to announce the coming of Yeshua, the King of the Jews.

The bride for several weeks or even months has had her wedding dress laid out each night besides her bed, so that she can get into it quickly when the midnight call comes. The bridesmaids too jump into their dresses and there is one mad scramble going on in the house. No doubt they have often practiced how long it takes to get into their beautiful dresses. They will have rehearsed things over and over so that everyone knows exactly what they have to do, working as a united team. They have only ONE HOUR, and it does not do to keep your husband waiting. Everything is ready and packed to go. THE ONLY WARNING THEY HAVE IS THE SHOUT!

"For the Lord Himself will descend from heaven with a shout, with the voice of an archangel, and with the trumpet of God, and the dead in Christ will rise first. Then we who are alive and remain shall be caught up together with them in the clouds to meet the Lord in the air. And thus we shall always be with the Lord."
(1Thessalonians 4:16-17 NKJV)

What happens when you only have only ONE HOUR AND YOURE not ready? We need to be wise virgins and have our lamps full of oil at all times. If you don't have any oil in your lamp, or you don't even know where your lamp is, the wedding party is going to leave without you. There were no streetlamps back then and probably no paved roads either. You would be very wise to have your oil lamps at the ready and full of oil otherwise you would not be able to see where you were going. It was an essential precaution, as the bridegroom would always come in the middle of the night so as to add to the surprise. You know he will call, but when is he going to come? Will it be this night? You've done everything. You've made a thousand and one preparations and now you simply cannot wait. When is he going to come?

Once the Bridegroom arrives the whole procession makes for the home of the Bride. Every one has their oil lamp and there are musicians, lots of laughter and singing as the happy throng gets bigger and bigger, as all the neighbours and friends on the way join in the procession. When they arrive the bride and the bridegroom enter into their new home and the wedding feast begins. A Jewish wedding feast lasts seven days, just like the Feast of Tabernacles. There is something about a wedding feast that no other celebration has.

The Wedding Supper of the Lamb

The Feast of Tabernacles (in Hebrew: Sukkot), sym-bolically represents the millennial reign of Messiah. The Wedding Supper of the Lamb ushers in this wonderful period of time. It takes place during the very first Festival of Sukkot of the New Messianic era. This Festival represents a Divine union between the Lamb of God and the harvest of the Firstfruits, and what greater cause could there possibly be for rejoicing for the glorious participants of the ultimate Wedding Supper of all time?

What an indescribable honour awaits those who are wise! Let us diligently prepare ourselves, whilst waiting in high expectation for that GREAT SHOUT – "THE BRIDEGROOM IS COMING!" This is the goal of our heav-enly calling. This is the goal of our discipleship! YESHUA WILL HAVE HIS BRIDE! HE WILL!

THE ONLY QUESTION IS – WILL YOU BE THERE
AT HIS WEDDING?

We are living in prophetically significant times. Of
course, there will be plenty of scoffers. There always are,
but to those who are given to understand the signs of the
times, they will know the course that is laid out before them.
The dawning of our redemption is even now at the door. It
has come upon our generation. Many of our Jewish brothers
are already returned to the land. For those of us who, like
Abraham, have come out of Babylon and returned to our
Hebrew roots, the time is drawing near for us to join our
brothers from the house of Judah. The call will come from
Judah; it will come because it is prophesied to come:

"In those days the house of Judah shall walk with the house
of Israel, and they shall come together out of the land of
the north to the land, that I have given as an inheritance to
your fathers." (Jeremiah 3:18 NKJV)

Yes, it sounds scary, but it can also prove exhilarating. We
did not choose to live in these times, but we must choose to live.
There will be a need for all of us, with all kinds of strengths
and gifts to contribute. Many will need encouragement, comfort, and help. Others will need guidance and instruction from
those stronger and wiser in the body. In the end the body will
come together and it will be fitly joined together. Will you be
the one from your city, or amongst the two from your family?
The choice really might just be in your hands

CHAPTER FIVE

"I WILL MAKE YOU FISHERS OF MEN"

The fish are the Lost sheep of the house of Israel

The beauty of the Scriptures is that the Bible invariably interprets itself, and this is the reason why we can never take any single statement at face value, as we have already seen with some of Yeshua's parables quoted in the previous chapters, there usually lays a deeper meaning behind the words both of the Prophets and those of Yeshua, our Messiah. This fundamental biblical precept is made clear by Isaiah, as he introduces the principle as follows:

"Who will he teach knowledge? And whom will he make to understand the message? Those just weaned from milk? Those just drawn from the breast?
For precept must be upon precept, Line upon line, Here a little, there a little."
(Isaiah 28:9-10).

Isaiah is emphasizing here that those who wish to understand the message in any given scripture need to search for it line upon line, and that they are not likely to discover the whole picture in one place because we find, *'here a little and there a little!'* For example there have been hundreds of different and frequently contradictory interpretations of the various meanings of the mysterious symbols expressed in the prophetic book of Revelation, yet without the vital input from the books of Isaiah and Daniel, matched with an understanding of historical events, it is not possible for anyone to make any sense of it. In short the Bible interprets itself and it needs to be seen as a whole. Oftentimes it can be equated to putting a jigsaw puzzle together and in this respect it really helps if you understand the overall pattern of the Father's plan for the salvation of His people. What is necessary is a good knowledge of the Old Testament, especially the first five books of Moses, which are the foundation of all that is written in both the Old Testament and the New or rather the *'Renewed'* Testament.

Remember, we need to always keep in mind that the Father is the God of Israel and therefore by definition His people are the people of Israel, and that ALL of Scripture is focused on that reality. Thus when Yeshua addressed His disciples with the words: *"I will make you fishers of men,"* the *'men'* He was referring to were, *those lost sheep of the house of Israel,* His Father had sent Him to save (Matthew 15:24).

The Bible is one huge jigsaw puzzle

When we examine the context of Isaiah statement about *'precept upon precept'* he was addressing Ephraim, the prodigal and wayward house of Israel, as is made clear in the first few verses of chapter 28. The prophet then goes on to explain that the LORD has turned His word into one huge jigsaw puzzle for a reason and that it is done by deliberate design. Isaiah makes this clear as follows:

But the word of the LORD was to them, "Precept upon precept, precept upon precept, Line upon line, line upon line," that they might go and fall backward, and be broken and snared and caught. (Isaiah 28:13 NKJV).

Basically Isaiah is saying that Father does not necessarily want *'them'*, e.g. all of His people, to understand His purposes at this time. Does this not also chime in with the words of Yeshua, the Messiah of Israel? Remember, He spoke in parables in order to hide the truth, as the true meaning of His parables was only for those who have been given to know, *the MYSTERIES of the KINGDOM.* (Mark 9:9-13).

Isaiah's words somehow connect also with the words of Solomon in Ecclesiastes:

To everything there is a season, a time for every purpose under the sun:
A time to be born, And a time to die;
A time to plant, And a time to pluck what is planted;
A time to kill, And a time to heal;
A time to break down, And a time to build up;
A time to weep, And a time to laugh;
A time to mourn, And a time to dance;
A time to cast away stones, And a time to gather stones;
A time to embrace, And a time to refrain from embracing;
A time to gain, And a time to lose;
A time to keep, And a time to throw away;
A time to tear, And a time to sew;
A time to keep silence, And a time to speak;
A time to love, And a time to hate;
A time of war, And a time of peace.

God's Plan of Salvation is encoded in His Holy Days

The LORD (YHVH), the Holy One of Israel, the Sovereign Creator of the Universe, has a plan for the salvation of His people Israel. His first priority is to save His nation, the *'chosen'* people whom He refers to as *"the apple of His eye."* Having saved and restored His nation Israel, His plan is to save the rest of mankind through His elect nation. His plan has several phases, which are encoded and enshrined in His Holy Days, with each day representing a major step on the way to its ultimate fulfillment. These Divinely Appointed Times represent the seven steps of His plan for the ultimate salvation of mankind, and their meaning can only be revealed by the Holy Spirit to those who in complete obedience consistently observe them.

It is a sad fact of life that Christianity at large has rejected those divinely ordained Holy Days, as being relevant to the Jews only, and they have come to refer to them as purely Jewish Feast days. This could not be further from the truth, as the Scripture is adamant that the very opposite is the case:

"Speak to the children of Israel, and say to them: 'The feasts of the LORD, which you shall proclaim to be holy convocations, these are MY FEASTS."
(Leviticus 23:2 NKJV, emphasis added).

Just a few verses further down in the chapter we find emphatic confirmation of which are the true Holy Days we are commanded to observe:

"These are the FEASTS OF THE LORD, holy convocations which you shall proclaim at their appointed times."
(Leviticus 23:4 NKJV, emphasis added).

The Scriptures are very clear about this, if you want to worship and honor the God of Israel then you need to observe His Feasts! The good news is that over the past three decades millions of Christians around the world have been drawn to start observing God's Holy Days, including His seventh-day Sabbaths, as they are returning to the Hebrew roots of their faith. It is a sign that the LORD (YHVH), the Holy One of Israel is drawing His prodigal sons to return home to the Fathers House. It is also a sign that we have entered the Age of Messiah and that His coming to establish His Kingdom is even now drawing near.

Yeshua came preaching the Gospel of the Kingdom

As Yeshua was walking by the Sea of Galilee, He saw two brothers Simon, called Peter, and Andrew his brother, casting a net into the sea; for they were fishermen going about their daily business. Then He said to them, *"Follow Me, and I will make you fishers of men."* (Matthew 4:19 NKJV). He then saw James the son of Zebedee, and John his brother and called them to follow Him also. Then in the next verse we are told the essence of the Gospel Yeshua had come to preach: *"And Jesus went about all Galilee, teaching in their synagogues, PREACHING THE GOSPEL OF THE KINGDOM."* (Matthew 4:23 NKJV, emphasis added).

Staying with the apostles for the moment, who and where were those *'fishers of men'* to fish? We have already answered this question in chapter two, when we looked at the commission the disciples were given, *"to go rather to the lost sheep of the house of Israel."* (Matthew 10:6). To get a further insight into the, *who* and *where* of those lost sheep, we need to go to the beginning e.g. the book of Genesis, where Abraham, the father of the faithful, is promised in a solemn covenant that his descendants are to become an innumerable multitude:

"Blessing I will bless you, and multiplying I will multiply your descendants as the stars of the heaven and as the sand which is on the seashore; and your descendants shall possess the gates of their enemies." (Genesis 22:17 NKJV).

This immediately raises the question; where is this *'great multitude'* the divine covenant speaks off? Israel today is a tiny country surrounded by hostile Arab nations. Only some five-and-a-half million Jews live in Israel, and the other Jews in the world number no more than ten million. Where are these innumerable multitudes promised to Abraham's descendants through his son Isaac? Surely a population of only some fifteen million cannot possibly count as being as many, *descendants as the stars of the heaven and as the sand which is on the seashore!* Even allowing for the use of metaphor or hyperbole, these expressions lead one to think of huge numbers.

Where do Christians fit in?

The Church has tended to spiritualize this promise away, by stating that the Christians are this *innumerable multitude.* Curiously enough, there may well be some truth in this, and stranger still, it is connected with a multitude of fishes! The answer is once again to be found in the book of beginnings in the place where Jacob is found blessing the two sons of Joseph just prior to his death.

"Then Israel stretched out his right hand and laid it upon Ephraim's head, who was the younger, and his left hand on Manasseh's head, guiding his hands knowingly, for Manasseh was the firstborn. And he blessed Joseph and said: God, before whom my fathers Abraham and Isaac walked, The God who has fed me all my life long to this day, The Angel who has redeemed me from all evil, bless

*the lads; <u>Let my name be named upon them,</u> and the name
of my fathers Abraham and Isaac; And let them grow like
a multitude in the midst of the earth."*
(Genesis 48:14-16 NKJV, emphasis added).

Joseph, who has placed Ephraim, his younger son
at Jacob's left side and Manasseh, his firstborn son at his
father's right side, so when he saw his father 'cross his arms'
to put his right hand on Ephraim's head, he was none too
pleased, and he tried to remove his father's right hand from
Ephraim's head to place it on Manasseh's head. His father
refused and then answered him with:

*"I know, my son, I know. He also shall be become a people,
and he also shall be great; but truly his younger brother
shall be greater than he, and his descendants shall become
<u>a multitude of nations."</u>* (Genesis 48:19 NKJV, emphasis
added).

So what does it all mean? To sum it up, Jacob speaks of,
An Angel or *'a Messenger, who redeemed him from all evil,'*
he then crosses his arms to bless the two sons of Joseph. As
he does so, he makes the sign of the pre-Babylonian Hebrew
letter *'Tav'* over his grandsons, which just so happens to be,
'the sign of the cross,' and in that ancient script it picto-
graphically means, *'seal, covenant, or sign of the covenant.'*
He then prophesies that they are to grow into a multitude in
the midst of the earth, or as the original Hebrew texts puts
it: *"May they proliferate abundantly like fish."**Orthodox
Jewish Artscroll Stone edition of the Chumash

Do the above statements remind you off anything? **Who
are these multitudinous descendants of Abraham, who
have the sign of the cross and the fish as their symbols,
and who speak of a Redeemer who saves them from all
evil?**

The implication we can derive from this is that Christians may well be numbered among the numerous descendants of those two sons of Joseph. Notice, that Jacob also emphasized that his seed would become *'a multitude of nations.'* This is translated from the Hebrew; *"m'lo ha goyim"* – meaning, *"the fullness of the nations,"* (e.g. Gentiles). In this he echoed the covenant promise YHVH, the Eternal God of Israel made with both Abraham and his wife Sarah. Yes, even Sarah, was promised that she would, *'become a mother of nations!'* from what we have discovered so far, we can reasonably conclude that those nations are likely to be Christian nations, who consider themselves to be Gentiles. Once again, we see that the premise that the Jewish people alone are all of Israel cannot be supported by the Scriptures, and it therefore cannot be true.

The apostle Paul spoke about the 'fullness of the Gentiles'.

The apostle Paul speaks about our time today when an increasing number of Israelites (e.g. Christians), who are having their sight restored; as they leave their ungodliness behind in order to return to Zion and the Hebrew roots of their faith. Paul explained that blindness in part had happened to Israel (e.g. Christians), until the *"the fullness of the (Gentile) nations"* (e.g. all of Israel) has come in. His words are as follows:

"For I do not desire, brethren, that you should be ignorant of this mystery (e.g. the mystery of the Kingdom), *lest you should be wise in your own opinion, that blindness in part has happened to Israel until the fullness of the Gentiles (nations) has come in. And so all Israel will be saved, as it is written: "The deliver will come out of Zion, and He will turn away ungodliness from Jacob; For this is My cov-*

enant with them, When I take away their sins." (Romans 11:25-27 NKJV, emphasis added)

Christians have almost invariably misinterpreted Romans chapters 9 to 11, for the simple reason they have been blinded to the fact that both the Old and the Renewed Testaments, when addressing Israel, speak of two families, two nations and two houses, respectively Judah and Israel. Christians have missed this because of their near 2,000 year old paradigm that the term Israel, equates to the Jews and the Jews alone. What Christian believers generally are unaware of is that it was Israel that walked away from the covenant, not Judah! Thus, when Paul in Romans 10:1 says: *"Brethren, my heart's desire and prayer to God for Israel is that they may be saved;"* he is not speaking about Judah, or the Jews, but rather he is addressing those wayward and prodigal sons of Israel, who broke their covenant with the LORD (YHVH). Furthermore, and in direct consequence they are also not aware that Paul was addressing them directly, as the Christian faith to this day has, much like their Hebrew ancestors before them, rejected the Law of Moses.

The astounding prophecy of Simeon

When little infant Yeshua was taken by his parents to the Temple in Jerusalem they met up by Divine appointment with a Levitical priest called Simeon, who pronounced the most remarkable prophecy over the Child. They had made the journey to have their firstborn son consecrated to the Holy One of Israel in obedience to the Torah, which instructs the following:

"Consecrate to Me all the firstborn, whatever opens the womb among the children of Israel, both of man and beast; it is mine". "That you shall set apart to the LORD all that

open the womb, that is, every firstborn that comes from an animal which you have; the males shall be the LORD's" *'And it came to pass, when Pharaoh was stubborn about letting us go, that the LORD killed all the firstborn in the land of Egypt, both the firstborn of man and the firstborn of beast . Therefore I sacrifice to the LORD all males that open the womb, but* <u>*the first born of My sons I redeem'.*</u> (Exodus 13:2; 12 & 15 NKJV, emphasis added).

To help us understand the context we need to remember that the term Israel in the days of the Exodus from Egypt was a term that applied to all twelve tribes of Israel. In those days, and right up to the time the nation split up to be divided into two kingdoms after Solomon's reign, the name Israel applied to the whole house of Jacob. However, after the separation between the two nations, the term Israel could only apply to the Lost Ten Tribes of Israel, who had forsaken the covenant and been scattered to the four corners of the earth.

We pick up the story in Luke chapter two, we notice in verse 21 that Yeshua was circumcised on the eighth day. Then some time later they took the Child to Jerusalem some thirty three days later (as per Leviticus 12:4), to present Him to the LORD, whilst offering, as commanded in the Law of Moses, *'A pair of turtle doves or two young pigeons'.* It was soon after this they met Simeon, who uttered the most amazing prophecy over the Child. We read in verse 25 that this man had been waiting for the; *"CONSOLATION OF ISRAEL, and the Holy Spirit was upon him. And it had been revealed to him by the Holy Spirit that he would not see death before he had seen the Lord's Christ.* (e.g. our Messiah). He had been led by the Spirit into the Temple that day and; *'he took Him (Yeshua, whose proper Hebrew name actually means 'salvation'), up in his arms and blessed God and said:" Lord, now You are letting Your servant depart in peace, According to Your word; For my eyes have seen Your salvation (Yeshua)*

which You have prepared before the face of all peoples, a
LIGHT to BRING REVELATION TO THE GENTILES,
and the GLORY of Your people ISRAEL." (Luke 2:25-32
NKJV, emphasis & author's comments added).

Here we have an example of an astounding prophecy
spoken over Yeshua at this most significant time in His
young life by Simeon, who was both a priest and a prophet,
who all his life had been waiting for the, *'Consolation of*
Israel!' It is so easy to read right over this passage but what
can it possibly mean? Remember, there was no Israel at the
time! This event took place in Jerusalem which was the
capital of Roman occupied Judea. The world in those days
was divided between two great empires, the Roman Empire
ruling over the territories west of the River Euphrates, whilst
the equally mighty Parthian Empire ruled over all the territories stretching to the East of the Euphrates. Israel had
gone into captivity seven centuries earlier, and there was
no nation at the time under either Roman or Parthian rule
calling itself Israel. The ten tribes of Israel, having departed
from the covenant by worshipping idols, had chosen to go
the same way as the Gentiles. Once we can get hold of this
truth we begin to understand the meaning behind those emo-
tive words which expressed the longing of Simeon's heart to
see; *'the Consolation of Israel.'* Clearly, Simeon, a *'Spirit*
filled' Levitical priest of the Temple service, was aware of all
the words of the prophets which spoke of the ultimate return
of the *'lost house of Israel'*. To him their return to both, the
Covenant and the Land of their fathers, would truly be the
'Consolation of Israel'.

Simeon in beholding the Jesus Child (Yeshua), who's
Hebrew name means *"Salvation,"* then goes on to speak of
Him being: *A light to bring revelation to the Gentiles, and the*
glory of Your people Israel." Notice, how Simeon, being led
by the Holy Spirit connects the *'bringing of revelation to the*
Gentiles,' as being equal to, *'the glory of Your people Israel!'*

Does this also not perfectly chime with the words of the Apostle Paul; *that blindness in part has happened to Israel until the fullness of the Gentiles (nations) has come in?*

Five loaves; two fish and twelve baskets – What does it mean?

We find another great miracle which Messiah Yeshua did in a deserted place near the city of Bethsaida. Yeshua (Jesus) had intended to have some time with His disciples privately. However, the crowd had got wind of where He was going and followed Him: *"and He received them and spoke to them about THE KINGDOM OF GOD, and healed those who had need of healing."* (Luke 9:11b NKJV, emphasis added).

Note, He did not speak to them about the *'Gospel of (Personal) Salvation,'* rather He spoke to them about the Gospel of the Kingdom of God! As the evening drew near the twelve apostles came to Him suggesting He should send the crowd away into the surrounding towns where they could lodge and get provision. They were without a doubt genuinely concerned for the welfare of the crowd, as they were in a truly deserted place. Yeshua, then told them:

"You give them something to eat." And they said, "We have no more than FIVE LOAVES and TWO FISH, unless we go and buy food for all of these people." For there were about five thousand men. Then He said to His disciples, "Make them all sit down IN GROUPS OF FIFTY." Then He took the FIVE LOAVES and the TWO FISH, and looking up to heaven, He blessed and broke them to the disciples to set before THE MULTITUDE. So they all ate and were filled, and TWELVE BASKETS of the leftover fragments were taken up by them.
(Luke 9:13-14 & 16-17 NKJV, emphasis added).

The question here is: Why did Yeshua perform this most extraordinary miracle? Clearly, from the text we can discern that He could quite easily have dismissed the crowd, as when His disciples expressed their concern for the physical welfare of the people, there was still plenty of time for them to get provision in the nearby towns and villages. Yet, understanding the utter impossibility of feeding a crowd that large, He just said to His disciples: *"You give them something to eat!"* The question surely is; why did He do it? What did He mean to convey to us? What is so significant about, *Five Loaves, Two Fish*, people sitting down in **groups of Fifty**, the food to be set before **the Multitude**, and **the Twelve baskets filled with the leftover fragments?**

Once we have understood the importance of the Torah, learned the truth about the Two Houses of Israel, grasped the sublime meaning of the number Fifty, and accepted the biblical significance of the Multitude and the number Twelve, the true intent behind Yeshua's miracle becomes crystal clear. The disciples most certainly would have been aware, especially, as they had witnessed their Master preach the Gospel of the Kingdom all of that afternoon. They understood that the symbolism of *'five loaves, two fish, the groups of fifty, the food before the multitude and the twelve baskets of remnants,* were no coincidence. They understood that the use of those highly significant symbolic terms had not occurred by happenstance, but that it was by Divine design, and they marveled all the more at the majesty of the astounding miracle they had just experienced. So, what can it possibly mean? What is the hidden message here? For us to understand the meaning of these symbols we need be aware that Yeshua's purpose is centered on the restoration of the Kingdom to Israel, as He is destined to become the future King of that Kingdom. Before we go into depth about the meaning the various symbols of His miracle of the feeding of the five thousand, let us first of all look at a brief overview:

'The Five Loaves': These loaves are simply a reference to the first Five Books of Moses, which are the foundation for all the Scriptures, both in the Old, as well as in the 'Renewed' Testament.

The Two Fish': Are a reference to Judah and Ephraim, the Two Houses of Israel, which have been so sadly separated from each other for the past three thousand years.

'The Groups of Fifty': The significance of the number fifty is that it is a reference to the biblical year of the Jubilee, the fiftieth year when all the captives of Israel will be set free.

The Food to be set before the Multitude: This refers to all the descendants of Abraham who are destined to be as many *as the stars in heaven and the sand on the seashore.*

Twelve Baskets of leftovers: The meaning of the *Twelve Baskets of leftovers* represents the restoration of the Twelve Tribes of Israel (both Judah and Ephraim) into one United Kingdom of Israel.

The above summary indicates that each of the symbols used in the miracle have something to do with the restoration of the Kingdom of Israel. When we remember that John the Baptist, Messiah Yeshua, the Twelve Apostles and the Apostle Paul all preached the same Gospel of the kingdom, it becomes clear that we need to look more carefully at these symbols to obtain the full benefit of true insight into their glorious meaning.

'The Five Loaves': These loaves are a reference to the Torah, the first Five Books of Moses. They are commonly referred to as the Pentateuch, which in the original Greek means *'Five Tools'.* The Greek Pentateuch perfectly reflects the true meaning of the much maligned word for Torah, as it in turn simply means *'Instruction.'* Our Creator, the Holy One of Israel, has given us those *'five loaves,'* as the most essential *'five tools'* for our special *'instruction.'* Because of historic anti-Jewish sentiment inside the Christian Church, most bible translations refer to the Torah, (*e.g. the five books of instruction*), as the five books of the Law. Whereas the word Law for many people has a somewhat negative connotation, the fact remains that the Hebrew word Torah does not denote Law. Thus those five loaves of the Torah are to serve as the foundational instruction for all the Scriptures, both in the Old, as well as in the 'Renewed' Testament. At the same time those loaves also represent Messiah Yeshua, Our Savior, as is made plain in the first book of John:

"In the beginning was the Word, and the Word was with God, and the Word was God. And the Word became flesh and dwelt among us, and we beheld His glory, the glory as of the only begotten of the Father, full of grace and truth." (John 1:1 & 14, NKJV).

The next day John the Baptist saw His cousin Yeshua coming towards him, and said, *"Behold! The Lamb of God who takes away the sin of the world!"* (John 1:29, NKJV).

In John 6 we find a parallel account of the same miracle where we discover in verse 9 that the loaves were barley loaves and that the Passover season was drawing nigh (verse 6). Yeshua had come to save His people by becoming the ultimate fulfillment of the annual Passover sacrifice. In continuing on the same theme John quotes the comparisons about manna being the *'bread from heaven,'* whilst at the same time giving Yeshua's response:

"For the bread of God is He who comes from heaven and gives life to the world." "I am the bread of life. He who

comes to Me shall never hunger, and He who believes in Me shall never thirst.'' (John 6:33 & 35, NKJV).

Our Savior was born in Bethlehem derived from the Hebrew *Beit Lechem*, which means, *'the house of bread!'* His mother Miriam laid Him in a manger which is a *'feeding troth'*. Can we see the analogy here with those five loaves? He is *'the Word that became flesh,'* and we are to feed on those five loaves, which represent the five books of *instruction* otherwise known as the Torah, e.g. the foundation of all Scripture.

Once again Yeshua emphasizes the same point: *"I am the bread of life!"* (John 6:48), and He then goes on to make one of the most controversial statements of His ministry, which even today is frequently misunderstood, and which in His day led many of His followers to turn away:

"I am the living bread which came down from heaven. If anyone eats of this bread, he will live forever; and the bread that I shall give is My flesh, which I shall give for the life of the world." Then Yeshua said to them, "Most assuredly, I say to you, unless you eat the flesh of the Son of Man and drink His blood, you have no life in you. "Whoever eats My flesh and drinks My blood has eternal life, and I will raise him up at the last day. "For My flesh is food indeed, and My blood is drink indeed. "He who eats My flesh and drinks my blood abides in Me, and I in him. "As the living Father sent Me, and I live because of the Father, so he who feeds on Me will live because of Me. "This is the bread which came down from heaven – not as your fathers ate the manna, and are dead. He who eats this bread will live forever."
(John 6:51-58, NKJV).

Upon hearing the above many of His disciples were offended and turned away. They had cried out earlier:

"How can this man give us His flesh to eat?" (John 6:52). However, the statement above can only make sense in the context of John 1:1, and the realization that Messiah Yeshua, Himself is, *'the Word that became flesh!'* He is therefore alluding to the fact that He absolutely epitomizes and represents those *'five loaves of instruction,'* e.g. *the Word of God in the flesh!*

Just as we have to feed our physical bodies every day to stay alive in the natural, Yeshua is pointing out here that we need to eat His flesh, e.g. partake of and internalize those *'five loaves of instruction'* on a daily basis in order to remain alive in the spiritual. He makes this point very clear as follows:

"It is the Spirit who gives life; the flesh profits nothing. The words that I speak to you are spirit, and they are life." (John 6:63, NKJV).

The Two Fish': If we base our premise on all that we have examined up to this point, and when we remember the overriding focus of Yeshua's ministry, the two fish in the miracle play a most important role in that they are a symbolic reference to Judah and Ephraim, the Two estranged Houses of Israel. These two houses which have been so sadly separated from each other for the past three thousand years desperately need their King Messiah, as only He can unite them once again into One United kingdom! The prophet Jeremiah speaks of this with sublime eloquence:

"Therefore behold, the days are coming," says the LORD, "that it shall no more be said, 'The LORD lives who brought up the children of Israel from the land of Egypt,' "but, 'The LORD lives who brought up the children of Israel from the land of the north and from all the lands where He had driven them.' For I will bring them back into their land which I gave to their fathers. "Behold, I will send for MANY

FISHERMEN," says the LORD, "and they shall FISH them; and afterward I will send for MANY HUNTERS, and they shall HUNT them from every mountain and every hill, and out of the holes of the rocks, "For My eyes are on all their ways; nor is their iniquity hidden from My eyes." (Jeremiah 16:14-18, NKJV, emphasis added).

Most Christians consider that these prophetic words apply only to Judah and the Jewish people, and insofar as Messiah's role is to reunite both houses of Israel, it is at least partially true. However, because they have mistakenly equated all references to Israel as applying to the Jews alone, they have missed the implication of this prophecy for themselves. They have been blinded to the fact that the long lost house of Israel is to be found amongst the bible loving part of Christianity. When Yeshua called His disciples He called them to become *'fishers of men,'* and, as we have already covered, He subsequently commissioned them with the strictest of instructions to: *"Go rather to the lost sheep of the house of Israel. "And as you go preach, saying, 'The kingdom of heaven is at hand.'"*

If you are a Christian reading this book, this prophecy is indeed for you and you are greatly blessed to still live in the time of the *'fishermen'* whom the LORD promised to send. However, time is even now running out for the vast majority of Christians, as a time is soon coming upon the world when *'many hunters'* will persecute the true believers in Messiah Yeshua.

'The Groups of Fifty': We find the clue in the words Yeshua used in addressing His own in the synagogue of Nazareth on the Sabbath day, as was His custom, when he quoted the words of Isaiah 61:1-2, which referred to His ministry:

"The Spirit of the LORD is upon Me, because He has anointed Me to preach the gospel to the poor; He has sent

*Me to heal the brokenhearted, to PROCLAIM LIBERTY
TO THE CAPTIVES and recovery of sight to the blind, to
set at LIBERTY those who are oppressed; To proclaim the
ACCEPTABLE YEAR OF THE LORD."* (Luke 4:18-19,
NKJV, emphasis added)

In short Yeshua has come to *'proclaim liberty to the captives, recovery of sight to the blind, and to set at liberty those
who are oppressed!* Who are the captives He has come to
set free? If you understand the Gospel of the Kingdom, and
if you remember why His Father had sent Him, those captives are The Lost Sheep of Israel, which, as we have already
seen, are mainly to be found inside the Christian Church.
They are *the blind ones whose sight* He wishes to recover!
So, where does the; *'Acceptable Year of the LORD'* come
in? Might this be the connection with the number *'Fifty?'*
Remember, the Bible always interprets itself, here a little
and there a little. We find the answer in the third, of the five
books of Moses:

*'And you shall consecrate the FIFTIETH year, and proclaim
LIBERTY throughout all the land to all its inhabitants. It
shall be A JUBILEE for you; and each of you shall return to
your possession, each of you shall return to his family.'*
(Leviticus 25:10, NKJV, emphasis added).

Yeshua, as we have already understood from His own
words to the townsfolk of Nazareth, He is the Jubilee, as He
and He alone, is ultimately the one who is going to set the
captives of Israel free! However, we are still speaking in the
future tense, as we have to wait for the, *"Acceptable Year of the
LORD!"* The comforting truth is that ever increasing numbers
of the true believers around the world are sensing that we are
living in those days, and that our generation will experience the
joys of the Jubilee in the Acceptable Year of the LORD!

So, what is the meaning of the *'multitude?'*

The Food to be set before the Multitude: Who is this multitude being referred to in this miracle, and where are they to be found? Again we need to go back to the foundational books of the Bible, as represented by the very first of the Five Loaves, to get our answers:

"Blessing I will bless you, and MULTIPLYING I will MULTIPLY your descendants as the stars of the heaven and as the sand which is on the seashore;" (Genesis 22:17, NKJV).

Remember also the words of our Patriarch Jacob, as he blessed Joseph:

"The Angel who has redeemed me from all evil, bless the lads; Let my name be named upon them, and the name of my fathers Abraham and Isaac; And let them grow into A MULTITUDE in the midst of the earth" (Genesis 48:16, NKJV, emphasis added).

The only question that remains is for us to establish where these Hebrew Multitudes of Israel maybe found? We find the answer in the dream our ancestor Jacob experienced at Bethel, when he saw the vision of a ladder reaching into the heavens with the angels of God ascending and descending, and he was given a direct Word from YHVH, the God of Abraham and Isaac:

"Also your descendants shall be as the dust of the earth; you shall spread abroad to the west and the east, to the north and the south; and in you and in your seed all the families of the earth shall be blessed." (Genesis 28:14, NKJV).

In the next breath the Patriarch Jacob/Israel hears the following prophetic promise:

"Behold, I am with you and will keep you wherever you go, and will bring you back to this land; for I will not leave you until I have done what I have spoken to you." (Genesis 29:15).

This promise did not just apply to Jacob personally, as indeed God did bring him back, but it applied to all of his descendants, as the context makes clear. Thus far it has been fulfilled twice already for his descendants from the house of Judah. They came back after 70 years in captivity to Babylon. Then they were driven out again in 70 AD by the Romans, and in terms of their nationhood, they only reestablished themselves in the Land in 1948. However, thus far the house of Israel has never been permitted to come home yet, those *lost, (mainly Christian), sheep of Israel,* currently spread out in the four corners of the world, are also destined to come home to the Land of their Fathers in their appointed time. The Apostle Peter in his sermon in Solomon's Porch referred to this whilst speaking of the ministry of Yeshua, when he said: *"Whom heaven must receive until the times of RESTORATION of all things, which God has spoken by the mouth of all His holy prophets since the world began."* (Acts 3:21, NKJV, emphasis added).

Twelve Baskets of leftovers: What is the significance of this? Again, once we understand that everything Yeshua said and every action he carried out all have exactly the same focus, which is the re-establishment of the Kingdom of Israel, everything falls into place. This goal cannot be achieved without Him *'proclaiming liberty to the captives,'* or without Him *'restoring the sight of the blind sheep of the House of Israel,* which He had been commissioned by His Father to seek out. Thus the *Twelve Baskets of leftovers* represent the restoration of the Twelve Tribes of Israel (both Judah and Ephraim) into one United Kingdom of Israel.

The prophet Isaiah repeatedly emphasizes that only a fragment, that is to say only a remnant of Israel will be saved. These are the ones referred to as *'the Leftovers,* (e.g. the remnant).

"And it shall come to pass in that day that THE REMNANT OF ISRAEL, and such as have escaped of the house of Jacob, will never depend on him who defeated them, but will depend upon the LORD, the Holy One of Israel, in truth. The REMNANT will return, the REMNANT of Jacob, to the Mighty God. For though your people, O Israel, be as the sand of the sea, a REMNANT of them will return; the destruction decreed shall overflow with righteousness."(Isaiah 10:20-22, NKJV, emphasis added).

Isaiah's use of the term *'house of Jacob'* here implies that he is speaking about the whole family of Jacob, e.g. both houses of Judah and Israel, that is to say, all of the twelve tribes of Israel. Yeshua, our King Messiah, is going to save a remnant – *the leftover fragments* – and weld them into the restored United Kingdom of Israel. This is in fact the very job description of our Savior, as the prophet Isaiah points out to us in:

"And now the LORD says, Who formed Me from the womb to be His Servant, To bring Jacob back to Him, So that Israel is gathered to Him, (For I shall be glorious in the eyes of the LORD, And My God shall be My strength), Indeed He says (to Yeshua), 'It is too small a thing that You should be My Servant to raise up the tribes of Jacob, and to restore the PRESERVED ONES of Israel; I will also give You as a light to the Gentiles, that You should be My salvation to the ends of the earth.'"

116

(Isaiah 49:5-6, NKJV, emphasis & authors comment added).

Thus we find that through the simply symbols Yeshua used in performing His miracle of feeding the five thousand, He was at the same time in the most subtle way explaining the Gospel of the Kingdom to His disciples. Only those who had been given to understand the *Mysteries of the Kingdom*, would have noticed the incredible connection. Having come this far, now you can too!

CHAPTER SIX

CHRISTIAN'S EMBRACING ZIONISM

Its origins go back centuries!

It is not generally understood that the origins of Christian as opposed to Jewish Zionism were birthed within influential Protestant circles in England and the Netherlands, as long as some four centuries before the foundation of the State of Israel in 1948. One of the very first exponents of the return of the Jews to the Holy Land was Giles Fletcher who was appointed by Elisabeth I, as her ambassador to the Tsarist court in Moscow in 1588. Moved by the plight of the Jews under Tsarist rule he published a treatise called; *"Dissertation on the Grand Charter of the Donation of the Land of Canaan to Israel",* which was published in 1591, and which today is held at the British Museum. In this work he quoted from the Book of Ezekiel Chapter 47:14, as it describes the new borders of the Messianic Kingdom to come:

"And ye [the 12 tribes of Israel v.13] shall inherit the Land: concerning which I lifted up My Hand to give it unto your fathers: and this land shall fall unto you for inheritance."

In his essay he also makes reference to the ten tribes of Israel and states that their return to the land is a Scriptural truth not as yet accomplished. He presents the *"probable grounds that the present Tartars near the Caspian Sea are the posterity of the Ten Tribes of Israel."* Fletcher was not only a statesman but also an eminent lawyer as well as a scholar of some repute, and it may reasonably be assumed that Queen Elisabeth herself was familiar with his treatise.

Those early seeds of Zionism had begun to take root whilst the long war of Protestant survival was still going on, and Christian Bible believers had begun to wonder what they could do to speed the coming of the promised Messiah. Their focus was on the prophecies in the books of Zechariah, and Isaiah together with multiple others which indicated that the Israelites were to re-conquer the Holy Land. They were excited to discover that the re-conquest of the land of Israel was spoken of by the prophets:

"For the LORD of hosts will visit His flock, the house of Judah, and will make them as His royal horse in battle... They shall be like mighty men, who tread down their enemies in the mire of the streets in the battle. They shall fight because the LORD is with them, and the riders on horses shall be put to shame.
(Zechariah 10:6, emphasis added).

The prophet Isaiah prophesied the rebirth of the State of Israel some 2,700 years ago, when he pronounced the following:

"Who has heard such a thing? Who has seen such things? Shall the earth be made to give birth in one day? Or shall a nation be born at once? For as soon as Zion was in labour, she gave birth to her children" (Isaiah 66:8).

This prophecy was fulfilled on May 14, 1948, when *'in one day'* the State of Israel came into being. Our modern history confirms Zechariah's prophecy above, as the very next day the infant State of Israel was attacked from all sides by five Arab armies, and *the LORD of hosts did indeed visit His flock, the house of Judah, and did indeed make them as His royal horse in battle...* Ever since that first victory over their Arab foes the young nation has had to fight off attack after attack from her Islamic neighbours and each time *they were able to fight like mighty men because the LORD was with them.* Although at times such as the Yom Kippur War it was a close run thing. The more recent skirmishes with Iranian backed Hezbollah terrorist's armies in the Lebanon, and the Mini war against Hamas in Gaza have not produced the unequivocal victories of the past.

The origins of Christian Zionism go back 350 years

Nevertheless, the seeds for the ultimate restoration of Israel were sown in the early years of the 17th century when Protestant Reformers were distributing Zionist tracts in England, Holland, Denmark and elsewhere. Their focus was on the Scriptures which showed how the return of the Jews to Israel would facilitate the coming of the Messiah. Their blind spot was that they, much like most Christian believers today, could not distinguish the difference between the house of Judah and the house of Ephraim/Israel. Apart from a few notable exceptions they were blinded to the distinction between the two houses of Israel, which prevented them from thinking of themselves as Ephraim, or indeed as Israelites. Nevertheless, their Zionism was down to earth having been honed through three centuries of merciless warfare and martyrdom under the terrors of the Spanish Inquisition.

In 1648, when the Thirty years War had just ended they saw the hand of God in their victorious struggle. In this war for religious supremacy five-sixth of all German towns and villages were destroyed. The Palatinate, in western Germany, was plundered twenty eight times, and a population of eighteen million people was reduced to a mere four million. The Spanish Inquisition, whilst still in full swing in Catholic territories, had been extinguished in the newly recognised Dutch and Swiss Protestant Republics. Estimates of the carnage of war and the resultant famines and pestilential epidemics were that nearly one half of the population of the Holy Roman Empire had perished in the multiple conflagrations. The Civil War in England too had overturned the natural order, which the shock execution of King Charles I, on the 30th January 1649, only served to underline still further.

Messianic fervour stimulated by the signs of the times

All of these momentous events were fuelling apocalyptic visions of a Protestant populace who had come to look upon the Pope in the Vatican as the Anti-Christ and at the King of Spain as the Beast described in the Book of Revelation. These assumptions were not without logic, as the Inquisition aimed to get rid of all Bible readers who were brutally persecuted, tortured, killed and had their works burned. It lasted over 400 years in Europe, and in the end they only gave up against these so-called "heretics" because they saw they had become to numerous to exterminate completely. Messianic speculation was rife with many Bible reading scholars and preachers becoming convinced that the end of the age was nigh. This expectation was considerably heightened by the appearance of a succession of great comets respectively in 1618, 1648 and 1652 respectively. The combination of all of these factors in turn led to a clamour for the readmission of the Jews to England. Fuelled by the Messianic fervour of the times, many zealous Puritan scholars had begun to study the Hebrew language in order to better understand the words of the Bible, and this same trend had been growing throughout Europe both in Protestant and Catholic circles. In all probability this increasing interest in Hebrew was at least partly due to the combative spirit between the two warring parties of Protestants and Papists, in which the language of the Patriarchs and the Prophets might be used as a weapon to justify their own cause.

It was natural for them to think of restoring Israel by force, as foreseen by the prophets of Israel. The Puritans, a Calvinist sect in England, were at the forefront of this fledgling Zionist movement, and in 1649, two English Puritans from Amsterdam sent the following petition to the new Puritan government of Cromwell's England:

"Your petitioners being conversant in that city (Amsterdam) with and amongst some of the Izraell race called Jews... by discourse with them and serious perusal of the Prophets, both they and we find that the time of her call draweth nigh; whereby they together with us, shall come to know Emanuell, the Lord of Life, Light, and Glory...for the glorious manifestation thereof and pious meanes thereunto, your Petitioners humbly pray that this Nation of England, with the Inhabitants of the Netherlands, shall be the first and the readiest to transport Izraell's sons and daughters in their ships to the Land promised to their forefathers, Abraham, Isaac and Jacob for an everlasting inheritance."
(From: Joanna and Ebenezer Cartwright, *The Petition of the Jews for the repealing of the act of parliament for their banishment out of England*, London, 1649, cited in Tuchman, pp. 121-122.)

Notice those Puritan Christians had interpreted the prophetic words of the Bible in consultation with the Jews of Amsterdam. Even though as Christians and Jews they made strange bedfellows, they had nevertheless concluded that after centuries of persecution inquisition and war, the time had come for Israel to be restored. Their motive was to bring about the return of Messiah. Even though as Christians and Jews they could not agree on His identity, they were at least able to share the hope of his coming. A huge body of literature on the subject was written especially in England.

Battle for the readmission of the Jews to England

One of the greatest advocates for the readmission of the Jews to England was a Scottish churchman named John Drury who had been educated at Leyden in Holland. He had been greatly influenced by the great orator and Hebrew scholar Rabbi Menasseh ben Israel of Amsterdam, and had become convinced of the fact that the Lost Tribes of Israel would reappear just before the millennium, which he believed would be ushered in by the return of Christ in 1655. According to Drury the Jews would have to be sought in every corner of the globe before the millennium, and he became one of the first voices clamouring for the return of the Jews to England. Menasseh ben Israel, a famous rabbi, wrote to John Drury on the 23rd December 1649: "*I think that the descendants of the ten tribes live not only in America but also around the whole world. These are those Jews who have not seen the second Temple; they, possibly, will be dispersed until the prophecies of their reunification are realised.*"*
(copyright 2003 NEW TRADITION)

This same Rabbi Menasseh ben Israel of Amsterdam was one of the most respected rabbinic authorities of the time, and through his many contacts with the Puritan divines of England, he constantly urged them to work for the return of the Jews to England. The Jews were suffering unspeakable persecution in Roman Catholic lands subject to the Spanish Inquisition, as well as terrible pogroms in the Ukraine and Poland, and Menasseh was committed to finding safe havens for fleeing Jews other than in the Dutch Republic. He was an exceptional scholar and a man of great renown who, as one of its three Chief Rabbis, represented the Jewish community in Amsterdam. The Dutch capital was being referred to as the Jerusalem of the north and in those days it was the centre of world Jewry. Rabbi Menasseh promoted the idea of the existence of the Lost Tribes of Israel, and in the Messianic fervour of those days it was readily accepted by many Bible scholars of the day.

As early as September 1651 he wrote to the Council of State requesting the readmission of the Jews to England. Then in 1655 he formally petitioned Cromwell requesting the same. Soon afterwards he was invited to England by Oliver Cromwell, the Lord Protector, to a specially convened conference at Whitehall in December 1655 to discuss this very issue. Whereas, the conference itself was inconclusive, the effect was that Jews were permitted to settle and trade in England from that time onwards. Oliver Cromwell, the Lord Protector of England, expressed his own thoughts on the subject of the Jews return to their Promised Land in a passionate speech to the Little Parliament in July 1656:

"'There (in Psalms) it prophesies that, "He shall bring this people again from the depth of the sea" as He once lead Israel through the Red Sea. And it may be, as some think, God will bring the Jews home to their station from the "isles of the sea" and answer the expectations "as from the depth of the sea"..."

What will be the signs of Your coming, and of the end of the age?

To add to the general despair of the times the Great Plague had struck England with a most apocalyptic power, as it stalked through London and the countryside throughout 1665. It struck London particularly hard, as by the year's end, some 100,000 people had died a terrible death. At the peak of the outbreak, the death toll in London alone had climbed to 10,000 per week. Normal life had virtually come to a halt in the city, with fear and dread stalking the streets. The royal household of Charles II had fled to Salisbury, only to have to move from there to Wilton after the plague struck there also. At the same time, England was at war with the Dutch Republic for the second time in a battle for the supremacy of the seas. In mainland Europe things were no different, and many saw these biblical calamities as a punishment from God, and as a further sign that the end of the age was nigh. All of them were familiar with the question the disciples asked of Messiah Yeshua; *"And what will be the sign of Your coming, and of the end of the age?"* The combination of plagues, famines, pestilences, strange weather patterns, wars and rumours of wars seemed to fit very closely with the answer Yeshua gave to His disciples in Matthew 24.

1666 and the Number of the Beast

Not a few faced the year ahead with great trepidation, as they were familiar with the Scripture in the Book of Revelation which gave the number of the beast as 666 (Revelation 13:18). The end of the world was widely predicted to occur in the year 1666. Their views were almost confirmed when the Great Fire of London began on the 2nd September 1666. Although the loss of life was fairly minor, the property loss was phenomenal. Some 480 acres, a full 80% of the city had been turned into a smouldering ash heap in the inferno that raged across the city for three and a half days. Tens of thousands were left homeless and destitute. All of these events only served to increase interest in the Bible and the Messianic Scriptures concerning the end times.

Those who held with the Bible noticed that the Scriptures spoke of the return of the Jews to their Promised Land, and this in turn became the impetus for the budding Christian Zionist movement.

Numerous English Bible believing intellectual scholars, such as the philosopher statesman Sir Francis Bacon, (1561-1626), John Milton, (1608-1674), the poet and author of the epic 'Paradise Lost', John Locke, (1632-1704), the influential philosopher, as well as the greatest mathematician and physicist of all time Sir Isaac Newton, (1642-1727), were Christian Zionist to a man. John Sadler, close friend and confidant of Oliver Cromwell, in his book: *"The Rights of the Kingdom"* (London 1649), drew parallels between the laws and constitution of England and ancient Israel. He went on to imply Israelite origin for the English constitution, and even inferred the English people had descended from Israel.

Sir Isaac Newton venerated the Bible and accepted its account of creation and in his later life he expressed a strong sense of God's providential role in nature. He considered his Biblical interpretations, especially in the book of Daniel, to be more important than his epochal scientific research. In commenting on the restoration of Israel, Newton quoted Daniel 9:25 in his work; *"Observations upon the prophecies of Daniel and the Apocalypse of St John,* which was published posthumously in 1733. The actual Scripture states:

"Know therefore and understand that from the going forth of the command to restore Jerusalem until Messiah the Prince......." (NKJV)
As Isaac Newton concentrated as to how this prophecy might come about, he suggested that it:....*"may perhaps come forth not from the Jews themselves but from some kingdom friendly to them!"*

Clearly, Sir Isaac was on the right track. History having run its course, we know the outcome. That friendly kingdom turned out to be Great Britain! Yet another great Puritan divine and mathematician of those days by the name of William Whiston, (1667-1752), prophesied how the Jews would be restored to their land:

"The first Return of these Jews shall be by ships, passing along the Mediterranean, from remote islands: which agrees to no nation so expressly, as to the British Nation."

These early Zionist visionaries were later joined by the great Christian revivalists and Bible teachers such as the Wesley brothers, C H Spurgeon, Bishop J C Ryle, and Charles Simeon. Many Christians were praying for the fulfilment of this vision, and prominent 19th Century politicians joined the movement for the restoration of the Jewish people to their Promised Land. Leaders such as Lord Palmerston, William Wilberforce and Lord Shaftesbury were hugely influential in furthering the cause for the Jewish people to be given their own state in the Holy Land.

A Land with no people for a people with no land!

This famous Zionist slogan was first coined by the Earl of Shaftesbury (1801-1885), the great English social reformer, who always referred to the Jews as *'God's ancient people'*. Like the Puritans before him, he believed that Christ's Second Advent would be ushered in by the return of the Jews to their Holy Land. He never had any doubts that the Jews would return to their own land, as he believed the prophets of the Bible. His daily prayer and hope, *'Oh pray for the peace of Jerusalem,'* was engraved on the ring he wore on his right hand.

One of his greatest achievements was to persuade the British government to support those Jews living in Israel under Turkish rule by representing their interests through a British Consulate to be set up in Jerusalem. In his view this was crucial for Jews to be able to return to the land and earn a livelihood. Shaftesbury's project was adopted by Lord Palmerston (1784-1865), who was twice Prime Minister and three times Foreign Minister of Great Britain. In 1838, he concluded a commercial treaty with the Sultan of Turkey that included the establishment of a British Consulate in Jerusalem. When Shaftesbury became President of the Palestine Exploration Fund, he declared in his opening address:

"Let us not delay to search the length and breadth of Palestine, to survey the land, to drain it, measure it and, if you will, prepare it for the return of its ancient possessors; for I must believe that the time cannot be far off before that great event will come to pass. I recollect speaking to Lord Aberdeen, when he was Prime Minister, on the subject of the Holy Land, and he said to me: "If the Holy Land should pass out of the hands of the Turks, into whose hands should it fall"? Why, my reply was ready: "Not into the hands of other powers, but let it return into the hands of the Israelites."

Shaftesbury's concerted lobbying convinced the government of the usefulness of the Jews to the Empire. He argued that supporting a Jewish homeland would keep the Jews on Britain's side. His persuasion had laid the groundwork which made the British government more open to the Zionist dream.

The power of the written word when told as a story

One of the top bestsellers of the 19th century was written by George Elliot (pen-name of Mary Ann Evans.) George Elliot is considered to be one of the greatest novelists of the Victorian era. After having published 'Middlemarch' which is considered Elliot's masterpiece, she wrote 'Daniel Deronda', which was published in 1876. The book deals with the relationship between Mirah Cohen, a poor Jewish girl, and the wealthy upper-class Gwendolen Harleth. Daniel, the handsome hero of this fictional story, discovers his Jewish origins and marries the beautiful Mirah. The couple subsequently travel to Palestine on an ambitious scheme to re-establish the Jewish nation. With Daniel Deronda, George Elliot proved that for her day a serious work of fiction was undoubtedly the most effective way of conveying a political idea. Towards the end of the story, Daniel Deronda exclaims the essence of what is on the authors own mind:

"The idea that I am possessed with is that of restoring a political existence for my people, making them a nation again, giving them a national centre, such as the English have, though they, too, are scattered over the face of the globe. That is the task which presents itself to me as beauty. I am resolved to devote my life to it. At the least, I may awaken a movement in other minds, such as has been awakened in my own.

Daniel Deronda was published in 1876, and it made George Elliot (Mary Ann Evans) the most celebrated pro-Zionist of the 19th century. Some years ago the BBC turned her book into a successful T.V. series which was broadcast on prime time T.V. and which was beautifully acted and meticulously executed in its period setting.

George Elliot may well have been inspired by some of the prophecies of Zechariah, such as: *"I will strengthen the house of Judah, and I will save the house of Joseph."* (Zechariah 10:6 NKJV, emphasis added).

Notice, how Zechariah describes those conquering Israelites as two separate houses, e.g. Judah and Joseph e.g. (Ephraim and the lost house of Israel)! Isaiah continues exactly the same theme as he prophesies that:

"He will set up a banner for the nations, and will assemble the outcasts of Israel (Ephraim), *and gather together* the dispersed of Judah.... *They shall fly down upon the shoulder of the Philistines toward the west; together they shall plunder the people of the east; they shall lay their hand on Edom and Moab; and the people of Ammon shall obey them"* (Isaiah 11:12 & 14 NKJV, emphasis added).

Important clue as to the identity of Ephraim

Especially curious is the fact that both prophets quoted above make absolutely no reference to the intervention of any foreign powers to assist the Jews in reclaiming their Land of Promise, and neither do they speak of any non Israelite power protecting them thereafter. They refer instead to action by the two houses of Israel, (Judah and Ephraim). This is highly significant, as they speak of a combined effort by both houses i.e. Judah and Israel. They do not refer to any other nations being involved! So the big question is: who has been working alongside Judah to put the present day nation of Israel back on the map and who has subsequently worked to ensure its survival?

Whoever they are, that body should be Ephraim! So what does history tell us? When we examine the record of history, we find the British together with their Commonwealth armies, at the forefront in assisting the Jews in their quest to return to their land, with the Americans coming a close second.

In this we are given an important clue as to the identity of Ephraim. Britain had been the first great power to recognise that the Jews had a right to a national home in Palestine and this right was enshrined in the famous Balfour Declaration of November 1917. Furthermore, it was the British Army, assisted by the Anzac forces of Australia and New Zealand, **including a number of Jewish brigades**, who liberated the Holy Land in December 1917. It was an extraordinary combination of circumstances, which led the British Empire, whilst engaged in a life and death struggle on the Western Front in the fields of Flanders, to send a huge army to the Middle East. Her geo-political objectives were to maintain access to her Eastern Empire, which was threatened by the German alliance with the Ottoman Empire. She thus sent an army of over a million men to the Middle East with the task of defeating the German allied Ottoman Empire, which in turn led to the miraculous liberation of Jerusalem on the 9th December 1917. For the Jews it was a day of special significance, as the city was taken, without a single shot being fired, on the eve of the Jewish Festival of Hanukah, which signifies deliverance, as well as light. Then in early 1918, the Turkish forces of the Ottoman Empire were expelled from the region altogether by the British Expeditionary Forces led by General Edmund Allenby, and from that moment on the door to Jewish settlement of the Holy Land was prised wide open.

The year 2007 marked the 90th anniversary of the famous Balfour Declaration of 1917, in which the greatest Empire in the world formally declared the Jewish right of return to Palestine. A year later, in 1918 Britain was given the Mandate by the League of Nations to rule over the historic Land of Israel. Churchill laid a foundation stone in Jerusalem for the Hebrew University, and stood publicly against the betrayal of Britain's promises in the 1939 White Paper. History shows how, after many setbacks and letdowns (including some major British ones), many painful trials and tribulations both within and without the Land, the Jewish State of Israel emerged from the ashes of the Holocaust in May 1948.

Thus the immortal words of the prophet Isaiah spoken some 27 centuries prior to the event had finally come true:

"Who has heard such a thing? Who has seen such things? Shall the earth be made to give birth in one day? Or shall a nation be born at once? For as soon as Zion was in labour, she gave birth to her children" (Isaiah 66:8, NKJV).

Ever since that auspicious moment, the new country had no truer friend in the world than the American people. It is a fact of history, that ever since the foundation of the State of Israel, the United States of America has stood by her as her 'big brother' protector. When we thus observe the joint involvement, first of all of the British and her Commonwealth brothers, and secondly of the mighty United States, we are given a subliminal indication of who '*the outcasts of Israel' (the house of Ephraim)* may be. We must also not forget that it was those same nations who stood resolute in a great alliance against the evil Axis powers, and it was through their combined strength that they were able to defeat Hitler's Third Reich. Even though they were not able to prevent the unspeakably brutal horrors of the Holocaust, they nevertheless were able to bring it to an end and thus save the remaining Jewish population of the world. As the saying goes, "Actions speak louder than words," or as the Bible puts it: *"By their fruits ye shall know them!"*

CHAPTER SEVEN

No. TEN REPRESENTS DIVINE ORDER

The importance of numbers in Hebraic thought

The Hebrew alphabet consists of 22 letters with each letter having its own numeric value. Just as each letter in the alphabet has its own meaning and sometimes more than one, the numbers too, each have their own significance. In Hebrew Numerology - Gematria is the calculation of the numerical equivalence of letters, words or phrases. Before we move on to the special significance of number ten, let us by way of illustration look at a few interesting examples by looking at the meaning of the numbers encapsulated in the names of the Hebrew patriarchs and the matriarchs of the Bible.

If you add up the number of Hebrew letters in the names of the patriarchs; Abraham (5), Isaac (4), Jacob (4), it adds up to 13. Then if you count the number of Hebrew letters in the names of the matriarchs; Sarah (3), Rebecca (4), Leah (3), Rachel (3), it also adds up to 13. Number thirteen just happens to be the numeric value of the Hebrew word *'echad'* or *'unity'* or *'as one'* and *'Avi'* or 'A*bi'* which is *'my Father.'* This is most interesting because when we add the total number of letters in both the names of the patriarchs and the matriarchs of Israel together, you get 26, which is the numeric value of *"Yud-Hey-Vav-Hey"* or Yahweh, e.g. the ineffable and unutterable Name of the God (Elohim) of Israel.

Ten is the number of Divine order, as we can discern from the Ten Commandments, the Ten generations from Adam to Noah and Ten more generations from Noah to Abraham. Ten is a number which has a prominent role in the Scriptures, where it represents the *"Perfection of Divine order."* It is the *"completeness of order"* because it marks a complete round. After ten, the numbers start all over again, as with 11, 12, etc.

Apart from the Ten Commandments giving us our Creators instruction as to how to live by His perfect standards, there are many other significant *tens* in Scripture. There is also the *tithe* or the *tenth* part of our increase that we are to give. The money for redemption was *ten* gerahs or half shekel, which was to be paid as atonement for one's soul (nefesh) at the time of each census, according to Exodus 30:12-16. Then there were the *Ten Plagues* sent upon Egypt that represented the full cycle of GOD's (YHVH's) judgment upon Pharaoh and his people, according to Exodus 9:14. At the time when the Eternal GOD made the covenant for the Land of Israel with Abram, in Genesis 15:19, *Ten nations* lived there. These included the; Kenites, the Kenezzites, the Kadmonites, the Hittites, the Perizzites, the Rephaim, the Amorites, the Canaanites, the Girgashites, and the Jebusites. In fact all the land between the River Nile in Egypt and the great River Euphrates in Iraq was covenanted to the descendants of Abraham, (see verse 18). This immutable covenant will find its inevitable fulfilment at the return of our Messiah when He restores the United Kingdom of Israel.

Then, there were the *ten* tests, or rebellions of our forefathers, the children of Israel, in the wilderness. The *tenth* rebellion involved the bad report given by *ten* of the 12 *spies* send out by Moses to spy out the Promised Land. We can read about the treachery and utter lack of faith by those ten princes of Israel in the Book of Numbers 13 and 14, as they stoked up open mutiny in the nation by their evil report. Gideon was commanded to destroy the altar of Baal belonging to his father, *"so Gideon took **ten** men from among his servants and did as the LORD had said to him."* (Judges 2:27). David was commanded by his father Jesse to take *ten* loaves and *ten* cheeses to his brothers in 1Samuel 17-18.

The 'TEN' TRIBES – How it all began!

So, how did all this begin and where did it all go wrong? We find the answer in 1Kings 11:30-31. Here we find Jeroboam, a prince of the tribe of Ephraim. He was feeling great because he had just been promoted by King Solomon, who had put him in charge over the entire labor force of the house of Joseph. Presumably, to celebrate his new found favour, he had bought himself a brand new garment and was on his way out of Jerusalem when he came face to face with the prophet Ahijah:

"Then Ahijah took hold of the new garment that was on him, and tore it into twelve pieces. And he said to Jeroboam, "Take for yourself TEN pieces, for thus says the LORD, the God of Israel: 'Behold, I will tear the kingdom out of the hand of Solomon and will give TEN tribes to you."
(1Kings 11:30-31, NKJV, emphasis added).

I dare say Jeroboam's reaction at having his beautiful garment (*might it be a Talit per chance?*) torn to pieces, must have ranged from profound shock to absolute elation at the promise of becoming king over the ten tribes of Israel. Then Ahijah, the prophet, went on to say the following:

'However, I will not take the whole kingdom out of his hand, because I have made him ruler all the days of his life for the sake of My servant David, whom I CHOSE (WHY?) because he kept My commandments and My statutes. 'But I will take the kingdom out of his son's hand and give it to you – TEN TRIBES.'
(1Kings 11:34-35, NKJV, emphasis & comment added).

In the following chapter we read how the final break up of the nation occurred. The irony is that it was all about money! The burning issue at the time was the punitive taxation policies of Rehoboam, the son of Solomon. The population of Israel was already being taxed to the hilt to pay for the lavish expenditure of Solomon's extravagant court. The tribes of Israel felt that whereas the tribe of Judah had proper representation because the ruler (sceptre), the royal Davidic line, came from Judah. On the other hand, they felt that in matters of taxation they did not have any representation. It was fertile ground for rebellion, as the majority of the people were not prepared to accept the situation. The ten tribes led by Jeroboam thus rebelled against the house of David, and ever since that day the two nations have lived apart, with each nation fulfilling its God ordained destiny.

The Scriptures both in the Old and the New Testament are full of symbolic references to the Ten Tribes of Israel, who having been taken into captivity by the Assyrian empire, simply appear to have vanished in the mists of time. They certainly vanished altogether in the minds of Christianity at large, but YHVH, the Holy One of Israel, has never lost sight of them, and He has repeatedly declared through all of His prophets that He intends to bring them back. So, let us look at some examples of these symbolic references to the *ten* lost tribes of Israel. For this exercise we need to use the number *ten* as our guide, as it represents the Divine order of their ultimate restoration.

Ten men getting hold of the skirt of a Jewish man

Perhaps one of the most significant examples is found in the Book of Zechariah, where the prophet refers to the people from the *Ten* Lost Tribes (i.e. Christians), approaching the people from the tribe of Judah by pulling on the skirts of a Jew:

Thus saith the LORD of hosts; In those days it shall come to pass, that TEN men shall take hold out of all languages of the nations, even shall take hold of the skirt of him that is a Jew, saying, We will go with you: for we have heard that God is with you. (Zechariah 8:23, KJV, emphasis added).

The reference to the TEN men from all the nations and languages appears to be an indirect reference to the Ten Lost Tribes of Israel seeking some sort of reconciliation with their Jewish brothers. Zechariah highlights the return of our Messiah to Jerusalem in verses 3 & 4 of the same chapter, and the term *'in those days'* has to be a reference to the end times! However, what does the term *'skirt of a Jew'* really mean? The NASB translation of the Bible mentions *'garment of the Jew'* instead of skirt, and this is a more accurate rendering of the original Hebrew. The Artscroll Stone Edition of the Tanach translates the term as follows: *"They will take hold of the corner of the garment of a Jewish man, saying, 'Let us go with you, for we have heard that God is with you."* Here lies the key to what Zechariah is saying. What typically Jewish garment is the prophet referring to here? To understand we need to go to the commandment given to the children of Israel in the wilderness:

"Again the LORD spoke to Moses, saying, "Speak to the children of Israel: Tell them to make tassels on the corners of their garments throughout their generations, and to put a blue thread in the tassels on the corners. "And you shall

have the tassel, that you may look upon it and remember all the commandments of the LORD and do them, and that you do not follow the harlotry to which your own heart and your own eyes are inclined, "and that you may remember and do all My commandments, and be holy for your God." (Numbers 15:37-40, NKJV).

The tassels or fringes are referred to as Tzit-zit in Hebrew and they adorn the corners of every Jewish Prayer Shawl or Talit. The purpose for these Tzit-zit on the Talit are to remind the children of Israel of the commandments of their Father. Each tassel or Tzit-zit has five knots to remind Israel of the Five Books of the Torah, whilst each also has eight strings pointing symbolically to Yeshua, the Messiah of Israel., as eight is the number signifying resurrection. Yeshua said: *"I am the resurrection and the life!"* (John 11:25). One of the strings is *blue* and this *blue thread* is known as the *'Shamash* (or Servant). The same word is used to describe the taller, centre light on the Menora (the Seven branched candle stick), which speaks of the Messiah. In the Menora, the *Shamash or servant light provides all the other lights on the Menorah.* Thus in the *'Shamash or Servant light,* as represented by the blue thread in the tzit-zit we have yet another reference to our Savior, Yeshua, who refers to Himself, saying: *"I am the light of the world."*

The strings of the Tzit-zit also symbolize our being bound up with our Creator and serve as a reminder of His commandments. When we take the numerical value of the Hebrew letters in Tzit-zit (fringes) and add the number five, (equivalent to the five knots), plus the eight strings, we arrive at the number 613, which corresponds to the number of commandments mentioned in the Bible. This explains the verse above, which says: *"And you shall have the tassel (Tzit-zit), that you may look upon it and remember all the commandments of the LORD and do them."*

The Hebraic view of the commandments is that they represent the expression of the Divine Will for His people. Just as with any loved one who clearly expresses his or her desire, we would naturally want to respond to their desire to please the one we love. The Hebraic way is to view the fulfilment of GOD's (YHVH's) Will as our way of showing our love of Him. Rather than the Law hindering spiritual closeness, it does precisely the opposite as it actually prepares the foundation for that special intimacy with Our Father in Heaven. The act of wrapping ourselves in the prayer shawl is therefore symbolic of wrapping ourselves in the will of God.

This puts a completely different light on Zechariah's prophecy that in the end-time there shall be *TEN men* (Christians), from all languages and all nations, who will take hold of the Tzit-zit (Fringes/Tassels) of the Prayer Shawl of the Jew, saying: *"We will go with you: for we have heard that God is with you."* The amazing fact is that this prophecy is even being fulfilled today, as many millions of Christians around the world from all languages and all nations are doing just this. By taking hold of the Tzit-zit of the Jew, they are in effect returning to the roots of their faith. Those roots are found in the first five books of Moses, which the Jews refer to as the Torah, and which, as the Word makes plain, Our Messiah Yeshua, observed in every detail, as they constitute the commandments of His Father. These Christians have come to recognize that when Yeshua addressed His *'chosen'* disciples, He said: *"IF you love Me keep My commandments!"* (John 14:15, NKJV, emphasis added).

As we have already seen in the 'Foreword,' of this book, the Hebrew Roots, the Messianic and the Christian Zionist Movements are an end-time move of the Spirit, which is sweeping over the Church. Those modern-day earnest disciples of Yeshua (Jesus) have come to understand that the Commandments of Yeshua, the Son of the Father, by definition cannot be different from the Commandments given at Mount Sinai. They base their understanding upon the words Yeshua spoke on this very subject, as He addressed His disciples:

"He who has seen Me has seen the Father; so how can you say, 'Show us the Father?' "Do you not believe that I am in the Father, and the Father in Me? The words that I speak to you I do not speak on My own authority; but the Father who dwells in Me does the works." (John 14:9-10, NKJV).

These Christian Israelites have also come to realise that at the time Yeshua spoke these words that the New Testament had not even been heard off. They simply had not been written. The Gospel accounts plus all the Apostolic Letters were just not available to the people being taught, either by Yeshua (Jesus), or by His disciples, for many decades after His death and resurrection. It is by common consensus amongst most theologians and Bible scholars that the 27 books of the New/*Renewed* Testament were written at different times by their various authors beginning around A.D. 50. The Gospel of John apparently was not written until around A.D. 90, nearly forty years after Yeshua's death and resurrection. Thus when Yeshua (Jesus) spoke about those who would truly love Him, their love for Him could only be manifested in them by the keeping of the commandments of His Father. Yeshua (Jesus) expressed it most beautifully and emphatically when He said: *"I and My Father are one!"*

The Talit – The Prayer Shawl of the Jew

In the Bible the Hebrew Talit is translated in various ways such as, *a skirt, a garment, a vesture, a cloak, a tent, a cloth, a napkin or even a handkerchief.* After the children of Israel came out of Egypt, each morning the heads of every household would stand at the entrance of their tent, covered in their prayer shawls, to pray. At the time of the morning sacrifice, they would stand in their Talits with their eyes focussed on the Tabernacle located at the centre of the Camp of Israel. Each man believed that the Shekinah Glory that dwelt in the Holy of Holies was taking place inside of him. Was it not also the Apostle Paul who said, *"know ye not that your body is the Temple of the Holy Spirit?'*

The Tabernacle at the centre of the camp itself was a large tent and the Talit symbolised the Tent of the Tabernacle. Thus the Prayer Shawl represents a miniature tabernacle! The Tabernacle in the centre of the Camp of Israel was made of white linen with blue borders and the cords at the side and the colors for the Talit are just the same. This leads us to understand the occupation of the Apostle Paul, whilst in Corinth:

"So, because he was of the same trade, he stayed with them and worked; for by occupation they were 'TENTMAKERS'". (Acts 18:3, NKJV, emphasis added).

The *'tents'* the Apostle Paul was making with the Jewish couple Aquila and Pricilla were almost certainly *'Talits'* for the Jewish and Greek/Israelite community of Corinth. Paul's occupation clearly had its roots in his upbringing and schooling at the feet of the great Sage Gamaliel. He would have found a ready market for his work in the thriving Nazarene communities of Corinth, Ephesus and Rome.

A further custom relates to the time when a Jewish man dies. His head is covered with his Prayer Shawl, because that way the temple of his mind is covered by the Talit, which symbolises the Temple and the Holy of Holies. On the day of resurrection the Holy Spirit of GOD (YHVH) will come and raise that body from the dead. The Talit is considered a Holy garment and therefore it is not permitted to touch a dead body. Therefore when a Jewish person dies, the body is covered in a shroud and his Talit is neatly folded and placed over his head. Does this not remind you of something we have read in the life and times of our Savior and Redeemer?

"And the 'NAPKIN', that was about his head, not lying with the linen clothes, but wrapped together in a place by itself. Then came in also that other disciple, which came first to the sepulchre, and he saw, and believed."
(John 20:7, KJV, emphasis added)

The NKJV uses the word *'handkerchief'* instead of *'napkin,'* when it actually refers to the Talit, which was invariably placed upon the head of the body. This is what made *'that other disciple'* (most probably the Apostle John), realise that His Master had risen from the dead. Once he saw that neatly folded Talit carefully placed apart from the grave clothes in a place all by itself, *"he saw, and believed."* Furthermore, we can find excellent confirmation for this premise in the account of the resurrection of Lazarus:

"And he who had died came out bound hand and foot with graveclothes, and his face was wrapped with a 'CLOTH.' Jesus said to them, "Loose him, and let him go."
(John 11:44, NKJV, emphasis added).

In this case the KJV uses the term *'napkin'* instead of *'cloth'*. Clearly both involve the placing of a cloth or napkin over the head of the deceased person, and once we understand the custom of the day, it can only point us to the Prayer Shaw which played such a pivotal role in the lives of the children of Israel. Many returning Christians today would not dream of visiting Jerusalem without purchasing a Prayer

Shawl for themselves. Understanding the deep symbolic meaning of the garment adds to their faith in the Master Yeshua, as they take their first tentative steps of walking in obedience to the Father.

A most powerful Messianic prophecy related to the Tzit-zit and the corners/wings to which it is attached, is found in Malachi:

"But to you who fear My name <u>the Sun of Righteousness</u> shall arise <u>With healing in His wings.</u>" (Malachi 4:2, NKJV, emphasis added).

During the time of Yeshua, those familiar with the prophecies of Malachi would have been waiting for a *Messiah,* who would bring *healing to many.* Malachi informs us that the *healing* would be *in His wings!* This same word is used to describe the *corners of a special garment,* i.e. the Talit. King David also points to the *wings:*

"How precious is your lovingkindness, O God! Therefore the children of men put their trust under the shadow of Your wings." (Psalm 36:7, NKJV).

Now picture Yeshua, the Messiah of Israel, and the Sun of Righteousness, wearing *His garment with the tzit-zit hanging from the four corners of His hem.* Surely, it is not too hard to believe that the people who believed Him to be the Messiah, the One who would redeem Israel, would *look for healing in the hem of His garment:*

And when the men of that place recognized Him, they sent out into all that surrounding region, brought to Him all who were sick, and begged Him THAT THEY MIGHT ONLY TOUCH THE HEM OF HIS GARMENT. And as many as touched it were made perfectly well. (Matthew 14:35-36, NKJV, emphasis added).

There is also the familiar story of the woman who had suffered for twelve years with a blood disorder of some kind who was healed by *touching the hem of His garment:*

Now a woman, having a flow of blood for twelve years, who had spend all her livelihood on physicians and could not be healed by any, came from behind and touched the border of His garment. And immediately the flow of blood was stopped. (Luke 8:43, NKJV).

Note, she touched the *border/hem* of His garment in Hebrew thought better known as His Tzit-zit, and that very instant she was healed. Afterwards, Yeshua commends her for her faith!

In those days it was the custom, when praying for the sick, to place the Prayer Shawl over the body of the sick person. In the Book of Acts we have the account of an amazing miracle by the Apostle Peter when he raised the widow woman Dorcas from the dead. The mourners show him all the tunics and garments, *(might these be Talits by chance?)*, which Dorcas had made while she was with them. Peter asks to be shown her body, and he:

Knelt down and prayed. And turning to the body he said, "Tabitha arise." And she opened her eyes, and when she saw Peter she sat up. (Acts 9:40, NKJV).

The term used here by Peter as he addressed the body of Dorcas, *"Tabitha arise,"* is an incorrect translation from the original Aramaic text, as the actual text reads, *Tabit a cumi,* which means, *woman in the Talit arise!*

Then there is also the account of those Roman soldiers who did not want to divide His garment, as a Prayer Shawl is made out of one seamless cloth, and Yeshua's would have been of exceptional quality, so they cast lots for it, just as King David had prophesied in Psalm 22:18. No doubt Yeshua's influential uncle, Joseph of Arimathea, would have redeemed His Talit by purchasing it with good gold coin from those same Roman soldiers, prior to the burial of our Savior in Joseph's own grave, close to the place of crucifixion.

Ten Virgins, Ten Minas & Ten Silver Coins

Returning to the theme of our chapter, let us examine some more New Testament examples, which indirectly point us to the *Ten Lost Tribes of Israel.* As we have already seen, in chapter four, there are the *ten virgins* of the parable in Matthew 25; five of which were wise and were prepared for their wedding. *Five* is the number of grace and, as we have already seen this number also represents the *Five* Books of Moses, or Torah. These *Five* wise virgins accepted the grace of Yeshua's sacrifice and followed Him. Just as He followed the Torah of His Father, so did they by simply walking in the footsteps of their Master, and in enduring until the end, they qualified to become the bride of Yeshua.

In the Gospel of Luke, Yeshua relates *the Parable of the Ten Minas* in response to the thoughts of His disciples, who were expecting Him to usher in the Kingdom of God at any moment! To help them to understand that He had not come to establish the Kingdom at that particular moment in time, He told them a parable indicating that they would have to wait a while:

Therefore He said: "A certain nobleman went into a far country to receive for himself a kingdom and to return." So he called TEN of his servants, delivered to them TEN minas, and said to them, 'Do business till I come.' "But his citizens hated him, and sent a delegation after him, saying, 'We will not have this man to reign over us.'" (Luke 19:12-14, NKJV, emphasis added).

Many Christian preachers have interpreted the latter part of the above quotation as applying solely to the Jewish nation, in that they have consistently been unwilling to accept Jesus Christ, the Christian Messiah. Yet, when we look more closely at the Scripture; *"But His citizens hated Him, and sent a delegation after Him, saying, 'We will not have this man to reign over us,'"* and we then examine the context where Yeshua called TEN of His servants and gave them TEN minas, the inference is that he is addressing the TEN *Lost* Tribes of Israel. After all, it was they who had broken His Father's covenant, and it was they who had left His Fathers House! Additionally, when we consider the only time Yeshua actually gave us the reason why He had come, He said: *"I was not sent except to the lost sheep of the house of Israel."* Clearly, Yeshua is not addressing the house of Judah here, but rather is speaking to His scattered sheep of the house of Israel!

We may refer to our selves as followers of Jesus Christ and as Christians, but what does it really mean? The Apostle John clearly lists down the distinguishing marks by which we can identify the true disciples of Yeshua, the Messiah:

"Now by this we know that we know Him, if we keep His commandments. He who says, "I know Him," and does not keep His commandments, is a liar, and the truth is not in him." (1John 2:3-4, NKJV).

This may sound terribly tough to most of you reading this, yet it is taken right out of the New Testament and, as we have already seen, it echoe's the words of Yeshua, our Savior, the Son of the Highest.

We find further evidence when we search for the hidden meaning in the Parable of the Lost Coin. In Luke 15 Yeshua relates the Parable of the Lost Coin, as follows:

Or what woman, having TEN SILVER COINS, if she loses one coin, does not light a lamp, sweep the house, and search carefully until she finds it?
(Luke 15:8, NKJV, emphasis added).

Notice, once again we witness this extraordinary and repeated reference to the number TEN! Truly, if we can but grasp the significance and the *Mystery of the Gospel of the Kingdom*, we will instantly recognise each reference to the number Ten, as being an allegorical reference to the lost house of Israel! Why? Simply because it is Yeshua's Divine commission to bring them back to the Father and after this to the Land. In the Bible silver as a metal denotes refinement and redemption and the TEN silver coins thus refer to the redemption of Israel. Silver invariably has to go through a process of refinement, which allegorically refers to the Father moulding His people through affliction. (Jer. 9:7; Dan. 11:35; Zec. 13:9; Hos. 1:10 & Mal. 3:3). There is also a footnote in the NKJV against verse eight which states: *'The Greek drachma, a valuable coin often worn in a Ten-piece garland by married women.'* Does this not remind us of the words spoken by the prophet Jeremiah to the backsliding and prodigal children of the house of Israel?

"Return, O backsliding children," says the LORD, "FOR I AM MARRIED TO YOU. I will take you one from a city and two from a family, and I will bring you to Zion. "And I will give you good shepherds according to My heart,

who will feed you with knowledge and understanding."
(Jeremiah 3:14-15, emphasis added).

The 'Ten' Lepers Cleansed

Another startling example of an allegorical reference to
the Ten Tribes of the lost house of Israel may be discerned in
the account of the astounding miracle of the cleansing of the
ten lepers. Yeshua was passing through Samaria and Galilee,
(e.g. the former territory of the ten tribes of Israel), on his
way to Jerusalem when He was accosted by ten lepers who
stood afar off:

*"And they lifted up their voices and said, "Jesus, Master,
have mercy on us!" So when He saw them, He said to them,
"Go, show yourselves to the priests." And so it was that as
they went, they were cleansed. And one of them, when he
saw that he was healed, returned, and with a loud voice
glorified God, and fell down on his face at His feet, giving
Him thanks. And he was a Samaritan. So Jesus answered
and said, "Were there not ten cleansed? But where are the
nine?* (Luke 17:13 — 17, NKJV).

Leprosy is a particularly loathsome disease as displayed
by the symptoms of running sores and malformed stumps. It
also manifests the most repugnant boils, scabs and ulcers on
the skin which leave its victims in the most piteous state. In
Bible times lepers were cast out of society, as it was considered highly contagious. Even today in the third world, lepers
are generally kept isolated in special leper colonies. Leprosy
is often describes as a plague, or it is even seen as a curse!
Lepers were considered unclean and as lepers moved about
the country side and they saw other people approaching,
they either hid themselves, or they would shout a warning,
"UNCLEAN!" In the Hebrew, the word for unclean is,

"TAH MAY," and it means, **defiled, contaminated, polluted, unholy and unclean!** The cause was contact with unclean things. (Lev. 7:10). When the Bible refers to unclean it is not talking about dirt that can be removed with soap and water. The key to understanding the meaning is that Our Father in Heaven wants His people to learn the difference between what is holy and unholy. He wants to protect His children from unclean things because they will *'rob'* them of His *'power, energy and blessing'* over their lives.

Leprosy is abhorrent to men and all society. Leprosy is deemed highly contagious. Leprosy disfigures and maims the body and eventually it kills!

Leprosy is a most potent disease which is symbolic of sin! Like leprosy, sin is abhorrent to God, our Father. Sin is highly contagious. Sin disfigures and maims the spirit and the body, and eventually it will kill both of them.

The Ten Lepers being healed and cleansed by Yeshua symbolically represent **the Ten Lost Tribes of Israel,** who have departed from the Covenant of His Father and have become steeped in idolatry and sin.

Just as the leper was put outside the camp of Israel, so also the ten rebellious and disobedient tribes of Israel were dispatched to the outside of the camp because the whole nation had become leprous i.e. steeped in sin, and they have since become scattered throughout the earth. The leper had to be put outside the camp in order to protect those who remained, and so it was also with the Kingdom of Israel, as sin is like a virulent infection, highly contagious. Thus in the miracle of the cleansing of the Ten Lepers, Yeshua (Jesus) was foreshadowing His future role of cleansing all of the Lost Sheep of the house of Israel from the ravages of sin.

So what might be the meaning of only one of the lepers returning to give glory to God and thanking Yeshua by falling on his face at His feet? Yeshua drew special attention to the fact by saying: *"Were there not ten cleansed? But where are the nine?"* The question is; what was He trying to convey to us? Once again the Bible gives us the answer elsewhere in the pronouncements of the prophets that only a tenth of Israel will be saved out of the holocaust of unprecedented calamity that is to come upon the world. This awesome time of trouble is referred to in the Gospel of Matthew, as "THE GREAT TRIBULATION!"

The Time of Jacob's Trouble

Just before his death Moses addressed the whole assembly of Israel with a particular warning about the evil that would befall them in the *latter days* (speaking of our time today). This punishment would come to them because of their wicked conduct. Moses called heaven and earth to witness against Israel (i.e. including America and the West in general), as he prophesied:

"For I know that after my death you will become utterly corrupt, and turn aside from the way I have commanded you. And evil will befall you in the latter days, because you will do evil in the sight of the LORD, to provoke Him to anger through the work of your hands." (Deuteronomy 31:29, NKJV).

The evil which is to befall Israel in the latter days is summarised elsewhere in the Bible as the *"time of Jacob's trouble"*. The Prophet Jeremiah refers to this unprecedented *'time of Jacob's trouble'* as follows:

"For thus says the LORD: 'We have heard a voice of trembling, of fear, and not of peace. Ask now, and see, whether a man is ever in labor with child? So why do I see every man with his hands on his loins like a woman in labor, and all the faces turned pale? Alas! For that day is great,

*so that none is like it; and <u>it is the time of Jacob's trouble</u>,
but he shall be saved out of it."* (Jeremiah 30:5-7, editor's
emphasis).

Notice that Jacob, (i.e. the twelve tribal sons of Israel),
have to undergo a terrible time of unprecedented trouble
from which he will, presumably after the nation has learned
its lesson, be saved. In case you wonder why this calamity is
to come to the United States and the other mainly Christian
nations, the Prophet Jeremiah spells it out very clearly, as the
people in his day asked the very same question:

*"And it shall be, when you show this people, (U.S. citizens,
as well as the Christian citizens of other Israelite nations),
all these words, and they say to you, 'Why has the LORD
pronounced all this great disaster against us? Or what is
our iniquity? Or what is our sin that we have committed
against the LORD our God?'*
(Jeremiah 16:10, NKJV, editor's emphasis).

It is a basic human trait always to want to justify one-
self. Note, that those people in Jeremiah's day were just as
oblivious of their utter degeneracy as the average citizen of
the United States today. The same may be said of all the
other English speaking countries as well as the nations of
north-western Europe. Jeremiah's answer to them is just as
relevant for us as it was for them, because it came directly
from YHVH, the Sovereign of the Universe:

*'Because your fathers have forsaken Me,' says the LORD;
'they have walked after other gods and have served them
and worshipped them, and have forsaken Me and not kept
My law (Torah). 'And you have done worse than your fathers
(ancestors), for behold, each one follows the dictates of his
own evil heart, so that no one listens to Me. <u>'Therefore I</u>*

will cast you out of this land into a land that you do not know, neither you nor your fathers; and there you shall serve other gods day and night, where I will not show you favour.' (Jeremiah 16:10-13, NKJV, editor's emphasis).

Moses has laid down what is in prospect for America and the other mainly Christian nations of the world. He has written a special summary of calamities which even now lie immediately ahead of our nations, (see Leviticus chapter 26). In this chapter Moses describes how after a time of continuing terrorism, devastating droughts, monumental earthquakes, pestilential pandemics and dreadful famines, the ultimate sanction for Israel's (i.e. *Christian nations*), disobedience comes into effect. This can be summed up as catastrophic defeat at the hands of military invasion forces, followed by enslavement and deportation by foreign troops who know no mercy.

This same pattern was set in ancient times, when in three separate invasions by the Assyrian Empire, the kingdom of Israel was expunged. The people were deported to territories within Assyria. This is the future prospect that awaits America and the other Christian nations. This future event clearly connects with the prophecy about **the Time of Jacob's Trouble**, the timing of which lies just ahead of us. Moses expressed it as follows:

"Therefore you shall serve your enemies, whom the Lord your God will send against you, in hunger, in thirst, in nakedness, and in need of everything; and he will put a yoke of iron on your neck until He has destroyed you. The Lord will bring a nation against you from afar, from the ends of the earth, as swift as the eagle flies, a nation whose language you will not understand, "a nation of fierce countenance, which does not respect the elderly nor show favour to the young." (Deuteronomy 28:48-50).

The Prophet Jeremiah points out how the wilful pride of Israel (i.e. *the Christian nations*), will inevitably lead to their captivity. In the passage below we discern the sadness in the heart of the LORD God of Israel at the prideful refusal of His people, *the flock of Israel*, to give heed to His warnings:

"Hear and give ear. Do not be proud, for the LORD has spoken. Give glory to the LORD your God before He causes darkness, and before your feet stumble on the dark mountains, and while you are looking for light, He turns it into the shadow of death and makes it dense darkness. But if you will not hear it, <u>My soul will weep in secret for your pride; my eyes will weep bitterly and run down with tears, because the LORDS flock has been taken captive."</u> (Jeremiah 13:15-17, NKJV, editor's emphasis).

Could it possibly be put any more clearly? This prophesied *'Time of Jacob's Trouble'* in Hebrew is called, *'Ha Tekufa haTsorat Yacov'* and pictures the darkest hour of Israel's entire history.

As the 10 tribes, who in ancient times seceded from the kingdom of Judah, are today generally to be found in the mainly Christian areas of the world, one can be sure that this ghastly tribulation which the Scriptures refer to as the *'Time of Jacob's Trouble'* is meant for Christians and Jews alike. This time of catastrophic calamity is also mentioned in Matthew 24 as a time of:

'Great Tribulation,' such as has not been since the beginning of the world until this time, no nor ever shall be." *"And unless those days were shortened, no flesh would be saved; but for the elects sake those days will be shortened."* (Matthew 24:21-22, NKJV).

Things will be so bad, that unless God Himself intervenes supernaturally, *no flesh* (animal or human) will survive! In the time preceding these calamitous days, many Christians, especially those who have put their trust in the spurious and unbiblical doctrine of a pre-tribulation rapture, will have their faith, such as it is, shipwrecked on the rocks of adversity.

The truth is that Israel and Judah, Christian and Jew alike, face this same terrifying prospect in the near future.

*"For behold, the days are coming, says the LORD, 'that **I will bring back from captivity My people Israel and Judah!'"***. (Jeremiah 30:3a, editor's emphasis).

This is speaking here of a release from captivity through Divine intervention for both Israel and Judah, which brings the *'Time of Jacob's Trouble'* ultimately to a happy end. At this point we need to realise a stark truth!

If YHVH, El Shaddai, the Almighty God of Israel, is to bring us *'back' from captivity*, we must first of all *go 'into' captivity*. This implies that the Christian nations of the West must first be defeated in war! It implies that the countries where the Hebrew sons of Jacob are presently located, (including the U.S.A.), will of necessity have to be conquered.

The Second Exodus

On the positive side, this Scripture indicates that all the descendants of Jacob, the Lost House of Israel, as well as the House of Judah, will ultimately experience a Divine rescue of monumental proportion. The prophet Isaiah emphasises that this Divine deliverance is the second time that all the tribes of Israel are to be rescued from the clutches of their oppressors. The first time was when YHVH, the Almighty Creator, delivered the Israelites through mighty miracles from their bondage in Egypt. The second time comes around after ALL of Israel has once again gone into captivity. Notice Isaiah's comment on this prophetic event:

"It shall come to pass in that day that the LORD shall set His hand again the second time to recover the remnant of His people who are left, from Assyria and Egypt"
(Isaiah 11:11, NKJV, editor's emphasis).

Remember, the *'first time'* was the Exodus from Egypt! Notice, that in the Second Exodus which is to come, only a remnant of His people, (*the people of Israel and Judah*), will be recovered. This means that the vast majority of Israel's population will perish through famine, pestilence, and the sword in the prophesied *"Time of Jacob's Trouble!"* Only a remnant will be left. The Prophet Isaiah emphasizes this point no less than four times in a previous statement:

*And it shall come to pass in that day that **the remnant of Israel,** And such as have escaped of the house of Jacob, Will never again depend on him who defeated them, But will depend on the LORD, the Holy One of Israel, in truth. **The remnant** will return, **the remnant of Jacob,** To the Mighty God. For though your people, O Israel, be as the sand of the sea, **A remnant will return;** the destruction decreed shall overflow with righteousness. For the Lord GOD of Hosts Will make a determined end In the midst of all the land."*
(Isaiah 10:20-23, NKJV, editor's emphasis).

Hosea was the final prophet to Israel before the northern kingdom fell in approximately 722 B.C. He prophesied that Ephraim, (*generic name for the 10 tribes of Israel*), would be punished and that they would end up in the land of Egypt.

"They return, but not to the Most High; They are like a treacherous bow. Their princes shall fall by the sword for the cursings of their tongue. This shall be their derision on the land of Egypt." (Hosea 7:16, NKJV).

Notice, that the first time the Northern Kingdom of Israel was taken into captivity, the defeated Israelites were taken as captive slaves to Assyria not Egypt! It seems therefore that in this second captivity the tribes of Israel may be taken to a different destination. Nevertheless, in Hebrew thought 'Egypt' is associated with captivity!

"Now He will remember their iniquity and punish their sins. They shall return to Egypt." (Hosea 8:13b, NKJV).

Egypt signifies captivity!

"They shall not dwell in the Lord's land, But Ephraim shall return to Egypt, And eat unclean things in Assyria." (Hosea 9:3, NKJV).

'Ephraim (i.e. the house of Israel including the United States) shall return to Egypt'. This can only mean a return to captivity and bondage similar to that experienced by ancient Israel. It would take the scourge of the Ten Plagues upon their Egyptian captors to bring about their release under Moses in the famous Exodus.

Many of the prophets of the Bible have frequently emphasized that at the end of the age Israel will once again go into captivity. As most of Bible believing Christians are part of the lost house of Israel, this means that much of the Church needs to face this most sobering prospect. Surely, this is unthinkable! Yet, America's unprecedented power is right now on the brink of collapse. The *'inconvenient truth'* for the American economy is the staggering mind-boggling size of the national debt. Total economic collapse is the immediate prospect facing the U.S., and the European Union is in the same situation. Once the world economy has imploded, violence and chaos will ensue, producing the ripening ingredient for absolute dictatorship, inevitably followed by war. Beyond this, the house of Israel is destined to go into the most savagely brutal captivity! The Prophet Jeremiah refers to a Divine rescue mission, as the GOD (YHVH) of Israel has promised to save His people from afar:

*"But do not fear, O My servant Jacob, And do not be dismayed, O Israel! For behold, **I will save you from afar, and your offspring from the land of their captivity;** Jacob shall return, have rest and be at ease, no one shall make him afraid. Do not fear, O Jacob My servant," says the LORD, "For I am with you; For I will make a complete end of all the nations To which I have driven you, But I will not make a complete end of you. **I will rightly correct you, For I will not leave you wholly unpunished."***
(Jeremiah 46:27-28, editor's emphasis).

The remnant of Israel is saved through a great Exodus. In fact it is just as the prophet Isaiah prophesied that: *the **LORD shall set His hand again** the second time **to recover the remnant of His people who are left*** (Isaiah 11:11), so the Bible states there will be a ***SECOND EXODUS!***

"But I will gather the remnant of My flock out of all the countries where I have driven them, and bring them back to their folds; and they shall be fruitful and increase. I will set shepherds over them who will feed them; and they shall fear no more, nor be dismayed, nor shall they be lacking," says the LORD.
(Jeremiah 23:3-4, NKJV).

In the First Exodus from Egypt ALL of Israel came out of captivity, whereas in the Second Exodus only a REMNANT will be delivered from their bondage. This is speaking of the *Second Exodus* which, much like the First Exodus from Egypt, will be accompanied by trials, by signs, by wonders, and by war. This is when YHVH, the GOD of Israel, shall save His people with a mighty hand, and an outstretched arm, and by great terrors. He brought them into the wilderness then and He is set to have them undergo the same terrifying experience again in this Second Exodus. The Prophet Ezekiel explains the scenario in vivid detail:

"As I live," says the LORD GOD, "surely with a mighty hand, with an outstretched arm, and with fury poured out, I will rule over you. "I will bring you out from the peoples and gather you out from the countries where you are scattered, with a mighty hand, with an outstretched arm, and with fury poured out. "And I will bring you into the wilderness of the peoples, and there I will plead My case with you face to face. "Just as I pleaded My case with your fathers in the wilderness of the land of Egypt, so I will plead My case with you," says the LORD GOD. "I will make you pass under the rod, and I will bring you into the bond of the covenant. I will purge the rebels from among you, and those who transgress against Me; I will bring them out of the country where they dwell, but they shall not enter the land of Israel. Then you will know that I am the LORD". (Ezekiel 20:33-38, NKJV).

Just as YHVH, the LORD GOD of Israel, addressed His chosen people, the children of Israel, at Mount Sinai in ancient times, the remnant of Israel of our day will have to undergo a similar experience after their great escape from captivity. We have already seen that this epic event is preceded by a climactic time of unspeakable trauma described in the Scriptures as the *'Time of Jacob's Trouble.* Sadly, most Christians do not see themselves as part of Israel. They feel that their inclusion is based solely on their faith in Jesus, and that such faith makes them 'spiritual' Israelites, but that it has nothing to do with genealogy. For this reason Christians have generally taken this term known as the *'Time of Jacob's Trouble'* to mean that this will be a time of unprecedented trouble for the Jews alone. The simple reason is that they have never made a genealogical connection between themselves and the patriarch Jacob. They have failed to recognize that whenever the Bible speaks about Jacob, it is referring to Jacob as a collective name for all the twelve tribal sons of the great patriarch, whose name was changed to Israel.

A Miraculous Deliverance

The 'remnant' of Israelite survivors is destined to be rescued through Divine intervention. The effect of their unimaginable ordeal in captivity will have greatly humbled and chastened them, and many will be numb with shock, as they are led out of their bondage in the *Second Exodus.* These survivors will be traumatised by war and devastated by hunger and disease. According to the prophet Jeremiah they will not be able to hold things together, because overcome with emotion, they will not be able to stop weeping as they come:

*"In those days and in that time," says the Lord, "The **children of Israel** shall come, they and the **children of Judah** together; **With continual weeping** they shall come, and seek the LORD their God. They shall ask the way to Zion, with their faces toward it, saying, 'Come and let us join ourselves to the LORD in a perpetual covenant that will not be forgotten. (Jeremiah 50:4-5, NKJV, emphasis added).*

The Prophet emphasizes once more the great majesty of this epic event which is in prospect for those shattered and shell-shocked survivors of the Time of Jacob's Trouble. The remnant of Israel will come with tears and with weeping and in desperate need of comfort:

'O LORD, save Your people, the remnant of Israel!' "Behold, I will bring them from the north country, and gather them from the ends of the earth, among them the blind and the lame, the woman with child and the one who labours with child, together; **A great throng shall return there,** *They shall come with weeping, And with supplications I will lead them. I will cause them to walk by rivers of waters, In a straight way in which they shall not stumble;* **For I am a Father to Israel, And Ephraim is My firstborn.** *"Hear the word of the LORD, O Nations, And declare it in the isles afar off, and say, 'He who scattered Israel will gather him, And keep him as a shepherd does his flock.'* **For the LORD has redeemed Jacob, And ransomed him from the hand of one stronger than he."** (Jeremiah 31:7b-11, NKJV, emphasis added).

Even though the prophets of Israel speak about a mere 'remnant' coming out of the tribulations of 'Jacob's Trouble,' the prophet Jeremiah nevertheless especially emphasizes that this *Second Exodus* is on a vastly greater scale than the First Exodus from Egypt. Most scholars recognize that the First Exodus involved approximately 3 million people, including the mixed multitude of peoples who attached themselves to Israel as they escaped from Egyptian bondage. The *Second Exodus* will totally eclipse the First Exodus, as it will be on a far greater scale, possibly involving numbers even in excess of 100 million descendants of Jacob. It will be on such a large scale that by comparison the First Exodus will pale into insignificance. The Prophet Jeremiah once again spells out the situation for us:

"Therefore, behold, the days are coming," says the LORD, "that they shall no longer say, 'As the LORD lives who brought up the children of Israel from the land of Egypt, 'but, as the LORD lives who brought up and led the descendants of the house of Israel from the north country and from all the countries where I had driven them.' And they shall dwell in their own land." (Jeremiah 23:7-8, NKJV).

This *Second Exodus* when *the LORD shall set His hand again the second time to recover the remnant of His people*, will be so great that no one will even remember the First Exodus (from Egypt) anymore. What can the above passage refer to, except the calling back to the Land of Promise of millions upon millions of Christians and Jews together? One thing is certain; the Bible speaks in this same context of the Messiah who will execute judgment and righteousness in the earth, and He will bring back both houses of Israel. Notice the words of Jeremiah:

"In His days Judah will be saved, and Israel will dwell safely; Now this is His Name by which He shall be called: THE LORD OUR RIGHTEOUSNESS, (YHVH TZIDKENU)." (Jeremiah 23:6, NKJV, emphasis added).

The clear implication to take from this is that both houses of Israel; i.e. Judah and Israel have had to suffer together in the period know as the *"Time of Jacob's Trouble."* The Prophet Zechariah also emphasizes that both houses of Israel will be rescued at this time:

*"I will strengthen **the house of Judah**, and I will save **the house of Joseph**, I will bring them back, because I have mercy on them. They shall be as though I had not cast them aside; For*

I am the LORD their God, and I will hear them. I will whistle for them and gather them, for I will redeem them; and they shall increase as they once increased." (Zechariah 10:6 & 8).

Note that the *'house of Joseph'* here is speaking primarily about the English speaking peoples of the world. What can it mean but the re-gathering of all the survivors of both houses of Israel? What can it mean except the rescue and re-gathering of all the Christians and Jews who have come through the great tribulation during that awesome time known as the *Time of Jacob's Trouble?*

In this same end-time context, the prophet Ezekiel also relates the glorious return of the captives of Jacob and the whole house of Israel. He emphasises that this event will only occur after they have born their shame and repented for their rank unfaithfulness:

"Therefore thus says the LORD GOD: 'Now I will bring back the captives of Jacob, and have mercy on the whole house of Israel; and I will be jealous for My holy name – 'after they have born their shame, and all their unfaithfulness in which they were unfaithful to Me, when they dwelt safely in their own land and no one made them afraid. 'When I have brought them back from the peoples and gathered them out of their enemies' lands, and I am hallowed in them in the sight of many nations, 'then shall they know that I am the LORD their God, who sent them into captivity among the nations, but also brought them back to their land, and left none of them captive any longer.'" (Ezekiel 39:25-28, NKJV, emphasis added).

Notice, that the final verse in the above passage makes it quite clear that it was God's will that His rebellious and unfaithful people go into captivity. This means that the end-time captivity of the Israel nations is destined to occur by His express design. It also shows that it is His intent to deliver His chosen people, once they have been purged of their rebellious nature. The good news is that they will be released from their captivity and delivered out of the hands of their enemies.

CHAPTER EIGHT

THE WOMAN
AT JACOB'S WELL

☙☙

A Samaritan Woman meets her Messiah

Once again we find a somewhat baffling account in the ministry of our Messiah that cries out for clarification. After all, did not Yeshua Himself specifically instruct His disciples NOT to go to the Gentiles and NOT to enter a city of the Samaritans? (Matthew 10:5). We might ask also, what is He doing talking to a woman who has had five husbands and who is currently living in sin with number six? We might also question why He saw fit to disregard the age old convention that Jews do not speak or have fellowship with Samaritans? Why was He friendly with this particular woman when he ignored the Syro-Phoenecian woman who pleaded with Him about her daughter? (Matthew 15:21-26). Why was nearly the whole of chapter four of the Gospel of John devoted to this particular woman? Might there conceivably lie some hidden symbolic meaning behind this woman at Jacob's well?

All of these questions may be answered by applying what we have already learned thus far about those lost sheep of the house of Israel, which Yeshua (Jesus) had come to redeem. It is important to notice the territorial connection here, as Yeshua had left Judea on His way to go to Galilee, which meant that He needed to go through Samaria. Both Samaria and the Galilee formed part of the former territory of the Northern Kingdom of Israel. It is interesting to note that virtually all of His twelve disciples came from the Galilee area also, and that most of His ministry time was spent in that area. A further significant pointer is that He came to a halt in Shechem, near the plot of ground that the Patriarch Jacob gave to his son Joseph. Furthermore, Shechem is located in the mountains of Ephraim. (Joshua 20:7). Therefore the place itself had a very special meaning for those of the house of Israel. Let us now look at the actual account of what happened after Yeshua had sent all of His twelve disciples away to purchase food:

"So He came to a city of Samaria which is called Sychar (Shechem), near the plot of ground that Jacob gave to his son Joseph. Now Jacob's well was there. Jesus therefore being wearied from His journey, sat thus by the well. It was about the sixth hour. A woman of Samaria came to draw water. Jesus said to her, "Give Me a drink." For His disciples had gone away into the city to buy food. Then the woman of Samaria said to Him, "How is it that You, being a Jew, ask a drink from me, a Samaritan woman?" For Jews have no dealings with Samaritans. Jesus answered and said to her, "If you knew the gift of God, and who it is who says to you, 'Give Me a drink,' you would have asked Him, and He would have given you living water." The woman said to Him, "Sir, You have nothing to draw with, and the well is deep. Where then do You get that living water? Are You greater than our father Jacob, who gave us the well, and drank from it himself, as well as his sons and his livestock?" Jesus answered and said to her, "Whoever

drinks of this water will thirst again, "but whoever drinks of the water that I shall give him will never thirst. But the water that I shall give him will become in him a fountain of water springing up into everlasting life." The woman said to him, "Sir, give me this water, that I may not thirst, nor come here to draw." Jesus said to her, "Go call your husband, and come here." The woman answered and said, "I have no husband." Jesus said to her, "You have well said, 'I have no husband,' "for you have had five husbands, and the one whom you now have is not your husband; in that you spoke truly."
(John 4:5-18, NKJV).

Here we see Yeshua (Jesus) coming to Shechem, the capital of Samaria. He comes to Jacob's *well* in the land that Jacob gave to Joseph. Can we not see that all of this has a much deeper meaning than might be apparent at first reading? So, what does it all mean? The Samaritan woman, is a picture of us (Christians) coming out to that ancient well for the wisdom of the Hebrews. Yeshua asks her to serve Him, and her desire is to do just that; so she gives Him water. She then observes by His clothes and His speech that He is a Jew, not a Gentile like her. She then expresses her surprise at Him being prepared to have a discussion with her, as she states: '*For Jews have no dealings with Samaritans.*' Does this statement not remind us of the Parable of the Prodigal Son? (See: Chapter Three). Remember, Judah, the other son, wanted nothing to do with his long lost brother, who used to live in Samaria.

She thus is speaking to Him about *this wall of separation* between her kind and His. He then tells her of the *"gift,"* that can only come through Him to those who thirst and wish to thirst no more. He is speaking about people who, *hunger and thirst for righteousness, for they shall be filled* (as mentioned in Matthew 5:6). Of course, this story is well known, but perhaps we have not understood that it is all about us.

Yeshua, then tests her by asking her to bring her husband and she says that she has no husband. He acknowledges that she has answered truthfully. The message here is that if we, much like those lost sheep of the house of Israel, are walking in breach of the Covenant of our Father in Heaven, by breaking His righteous commandments, we too indeed have no husband.

Yeshua (Jesus) then goes on to speak about her *"five former husbands,"* that she once was married to, as she was once married to the *"Five Books of Moses,"* the Torah. Now she lives in idolatry/adultery, having no husband, no covering and no redemption. In this He was affirming her ancestry, as a daughter of the Covenant, and the offspring of Jacob. Her fathers at one time on that awesome day had stood at the foot of Mount Sinai and they, together with all the other men of the tribes of Israel, had responded of one accord to the Law of Moses with: *"All that the LORD has spoken we will do."* (Exodus 19:3-8). All twelve tribes descended from the twelve sons of Jacob/Israel formally accepted the covenant, not once, not twice, but THREE TIMES, as they stood before the smoking Mountain. In accepting the Covenant her ancestral fathers had spoken for all of their descendants, as the Covenant of Sinai was made with the whole nation of Israel i.e. all Twelve Tribes. The promise of the Eternal Creator to His *'chosen'* nation Israel was couched in the most absolute terms:

"Now therefore, if you will indeed obey My voice and keep My covenant, then you shall be a special treasure to Me above all people; for all the earth is Mine. And you shall be to Me a kingdom of priests and a holy nation." (Exodus 19:5-6, NKJV).

They were to become a *kingdom of priests* – the word priest or (Hebrew: *kohanim)* in the context means that the entire nation of Israel is to be dedicated to leading other nations towards an understanding and acceptance of Torah. In other words Israel is given a divine mission. They are to become a *holy nation,* that is a people *set apart* from the rest of the world. The Covenant YHVH, the Holy One of Israel, made with the children of Israel (*all twelve tribes*), was in effect *a marriage covenant.* When the ten tribes rebelled against the house of David and set up their own nation they broke this *Divine Marriage Contract*, in that they turned their backs on the God of Israel, and went headlong into idolatry by worshipping other gods. This is why Yeshua spoke to this Samaritan woman about her *five former husbands,* and He did this in an allegorical reference to *Five Books of Moses,* which constituted the terms of Israel's *Divine Marriage Contract with YHVH,* commonly referred to as the Old Covenant.

The reason Yeshua addressed this woman was because he recognised her as being one of those lost sheep of Israel that He had come to save. In this case He did not refuse to speak to her, as he did to the Syro-Phoenecian woman from Canaan, who was pleading for help for her daughter in Matthew 15:22-28. In contrast Yeshua was much friendlier with this woman at Jacob's well in Samaria. Neither did He rely on the excuse that Jews had no dealings with Samaritans. Clearly, He invested His precious time with this woman because He recognised that she was one of those *'lost sheep of Israel'* that His Father had sent Him to save.

The Woman at Jacob's Well
is a Symbol of the Body of Messiah

What was also remarkable was that He had started the conversation, much to the amazement of His disciples (verse 27). We have seen that the city of Shechem, the area of Samaria, and in particular Jacob's well, all held special significance for those lost sheep of the house of Israel. Could it be that this woman at Jacob's well signifies something more than just a chance encounter between her and Yeshua, our Savior? In the Bible a woman is often used as a symbol of Israel. Might this woman at Jacob's well perchance represent an allegorical type of the whole of the ten tribes which had departed from His Father's Covenant with the nation of Israel? We find considerable evidence in the Scriptures that this may well be the case. The prophet Jeremiah states:

"I have likened the daughter of Zion to a comely and delicate woman."
(Jeremiah 6:2).

The Prophet also, in a reference to the spotless Bride of Messiah, composed of the redeemed remnant of Israel writes:

"Turn back, O virgin of Israel, Turn back to these your cities. How long will you gad about, O you backsliding daughter? For the LORD has created a new thing in the earth – a woman shall encompass a man." (Jeremiah 31:21b-22, NKJV).

The woman doing the pursuing is Israel, whilst the man being encompassed is Messiah Yeshua, the Redeemer and Savior of Israel. Thus the idea that this woman at Jacob's well is an allegorical symbol of the redeemed remnant of the lost house of Israel may not be that far fetched. We find further powerful confirmation of this allegory in the Book of Revelation:

"Now a great sign appeared in heaven: a woman clothed with the sun, with the moon under her feet, and on her head a garland of twelve stars." (Revelation 12:1, NKJV).

Then in verse 6, this same woman had to flee: *"Then the woman fled into the wilderness, where she had a place pre-*

pared by God, that they should feed her there one thousand two hundred and sixty days." (Revelation 12:6, NKJV).

Thus for three and a half years this woman will be protected in her place of safety, however, the enemy will then make war on her set apart offspring, who, will stand out in this sin-sick world like a sore thumb, in that they are recognised by something they do:

"And the dragon was enraged with the woman, and he went to make war with the rest of her offspring, (many in the Christian Church), *who KEEP THE COMMANDMENTS OF GOD and have the testimony of Jesus Christ."* (Revelation 12:17, NKJV, emphasis &comment added).

People who keep the Commandments of God will always be persecuted because mankind at heart is rebellious and does not want to submit or comply. Man is a lawless creature who does not wish to be reminded of the Commandments of God and tends to despise the people who do observe them, simply because they put him in a bad light. Man does not wish to choose the Tree of Life, as man rather chooses the Tree of Human Experimentation.

The woman at Jacob's well clearly signifies more than just an incident in the life of our Savior. Yeshua's contact with her patently is intended to convey a most important message to the house of Israel, as may also be gleaned from the remarkable amount of space devoted to the incident, namely some 42 verses in John chapter four. As Yeshua continues His discussion with the Samaritan woman He tells her that she does not know what she is worshipping and then He tells her about His *'gift'* and refers indirectly to the *Renewal of the Old Covenant.*

The woman said to Him, "Sir, I perceive that You are a prophet. "Our fathers worshipped on this mountain, (Mount Gerizim, the Biblical Mount of Blessing), and you Jews say that in Jerusalem is the place where one ought to worship." Jesus said to her, "Woman, believe Me, the hour is coming when you will neither on this mountain, nor in Jerusalem, worship the Father. "You worship what you do not know; we know what we worship, FOR SALVATION IS OF THE JEWS. "But the hour is coming, and now is, when the true worshippers will worship the Father in spirit and truth; for the Father is seeking such to worship Him. God is Spirit, and those who worship Him must worship Him in spirit and truth."
(John 4:19-24, NKJV, emphasis added).

Much of the Church is like this woman, as they too have worshipped that which they do not know. Like this woman, they too have rejected the Five Books of Moses, which contain the *Terms of the Divine Marriage Covenant.* Like this woman much of the Church also once had *five husbands* and is currently unmarried and living in sin. When Yeshua said, *Salvation is of the Jews,* He is not speaking of Judaism today. He is speaking of Himself as the Jewish Messiah of Israel, who is leading His ''lost sheep' to return to a 'Renewed' Covenant through Spirit led and Torah based worship, which acknowledges Yeshua as their Messiah.

The Old Covenant is 'Renewed!'

We need to keep in mind that the Old Covenant is a National Covenant which God made with the Nation of Israel. The Old Covenant was and still is a National Covenant which YHVH, the GOD of Abraham, Isaac and Jacob, covenanted with the children of Israel at Mount Sinai, when Israel was first established as a Nation on the

Day of Pentecost (*Shavuot in Hebrew*). The fact that the Old Covenant had to be *'Renewed'* does not take away the fundamental issue that it still is a National Covenant with the Nation of Israel. For example, if one has an old vintage car, which because of age needs a refit and some restoration, once the work has been carried out, it would still be the same old car. It may have been resprayed and given a fresh color, you may have added some new features, whilst servicing the engine, but it is still the same old car. So it is also with the Old Covenant. The idea that there are two covenants does not tie in with the Scriptures. The Apostle Paul makes this clear as he quotes directly from the Old Covenant/Testament Book of Jeremiah:

"I will make a new covenant with the house of Israel and with the house of Judah – "not according to the covenant that I made with their fathers in the day when I took them by the hand to lead them out of the land of Egypt; because they did not continue in My covenant, and I disregarded them, says the LORD."
(Hebrews 8:8, NKJV).

Note that the text speaks of a new covenant with the house of Israel and the house of Judah. This shows that the new covenant is still a National Covenant i.e. it only involves Israel. No other nation or people are mentioned. The Scripture also shows the reason why the Old Covenant had to be made anew, because they had disregarded the covenant and Israel was cut off and removed from the Land of Promise. The Old Covenant was not faultless, because no matter how religiously people observed the terms, as written in the Torah contract, it alone could not provide *eternal salvation* which *was first offered to man in the Garden of Eden through the Tree of Life.*

Many Bible teachers maintain that the sign of the New/ Renewed Covenant is the giving of the Holy Sprit, which fell on the disciples of Yeshua on the Day of Pentecost. However, Yeshua appears to contradict this premise, as when He was gathered with His twelve disciples on the night before the Passover, He said to them:

"For this is My blood of the new covenant, which is shed for many for the remission of sins." (Matthew 26:28, NKJV). At the Jewish Passover Seder it is called, *the Cup of Redemption,* and it is *the Third Cup of the Passover Seder.*

The content of this Renewed Covenant is confirmed by the Apostle Paul, as he once again repeats the prophetic words of the Prophet Jeremiah:

"For this is the covenant that I will make with the house of Israel after those days, says the LORD: I will put My laws in their mind and write them on their hearts; and I will be their God, and they shall be MY people. (Hebrews 8:10, NKJV).

Notice, this new or renewed covenant is made with the house of Israel! It is still a National Covenant with His chosen nation. Then YHVH says, *'I will put My laws in their mind and write them on their hearts!'* What laws are these? How many sets of laws does the God of Israel have? Clearly, those laws are the same laws or instructions we find in the Old Covenant, only this time He is going to *put His laws in their minds and write them on their hearts.* How does He do it? He does it through the *gift* of His Holy Spirit.

The Prophet Jeremiah includes a key phrase in his prophetic statement, which the Apostle Paul omitted Hebrews 8:8. It reads as follows:

"…..to lead them out of the land of Egypt, My covenant which they broke, though I was A HUSBAND TO THEM, says the LORD."
(Jeremiah 31:32b, NKJV, emphasis added).

Once again we discover that the Covenant God had with Israel was *a marriage covenant!* Can we also not discern from both of these texts above how much YHVH, the Holy and Eternal God of Israel yearns to have a relationship with His people? However, His terms are contained in those Five Books of Moses and the relationship can only blossom and grow through obedience. Logic alone should tell us that it would not be possible for us to be at one with our Father in Heaven if we wilfully refuse to live by His standards! The Apostle Paul in addressing the community of believers in Ephesus speaks about the bride of Messiah:

"That He might present her to Himself a glorious church (BRIDE), not having spot or wrinkle or any such thing, but that she should be holy and without blemish."
(Eph 5:27, NKJV, emphasis added).

Both the Apostle Paul and the Prophet Jeremiah are of one mind, as they are speaking of a time when the much heralded reunification of the Two Houses of Israel finally takes place. This is also where the heart of YHVH, the Holy One of Israel, is right now, because this restoration has to take place before His Kingdom can be established upon the earth. This is the time when our King Messiah Yeshua, shall marry His spotless bride. Paul speaks about this more than once, as he has devoted three whole chapters to this very same subject in his letter to the Romans. His words can best be summarised by:

"And so ALL Israel will be saved," as it is written: "The deliverer will come out of Zion, and He will turn away ungodliness from Jacob. For this is my covenant with them, when I take away their sins." (Romans 11:26-27, NKJV, emphasis added).

Paul is speaking here about a yet future time when all the sons of Jacob, that is to say, *all of the tribes of Israel,* will be back together in *one nation over which Yeshua, the Son of David, is destined to reign, as King of kings and Lord of lords.*

This is the glorious news of the Kingdom of God! According to Strong's Concordance of the Bible, the New Testament alone contains some 155 references to the Kingdom, the Kingdom of God or the Kingdom of heaven. As we have seen many of the parables and miracles of Yeshua are about that same Kingdom over which He is going to ulti-mately rule. Why is it that so many in the Church have not understood the Mysteries of the Kingdom? Why have they not understood that it is all about Israel?

CHAPTER NINE

REPLACEMENT THEOLOGY IS A SIGN TOO!

Replacement Theology – what does it mean?

The reason the Church at large has missed the fact that the Bible's focus is totally centered upon the nation of Israel, is due to the doctrine of Replacement Theology, which for centuries has permeated every facet of Christian teaching. This is also the reason why the Church has failed to understand *'Mystery of the Kingdom of God'*, which Our Savior so powerfully outlined to His *'chosen'* disciples in many of His parables. This mystery involves the bringing together of Christians and Jews, who between them represent the Two Faces of Israel.

Christian Church teaching for over 1,700 years has embraced 'Replacement Theology'. What does replacement theology mean? What exactly is its doctrine? According to this doctrine the Church rivals Israel by claiming that she is the *"New Israel of the Spirit"* superseding the *"old Israel of the flesh"*. It is a claim which stresses the Church's superiority over the common Jew! This incredibly arrogant claim of the Church found its legal expressions in the *"Codex*

*Justinian",*which subsequently spawned the Inquisition, the Crusades, as well as multiple expulsions and pogroms of the Jews, who were seen as the Christ killers! Today we see this theory manifest itself by calling for "even-handedness" in the Arab/Israel dispute. According to this theory, the Jews are held solely responsible for the murder of Christ, the Christian Messiah, and consequently, all of God's promises to *'physical'* Israel have been cancelled, as they have been transferred to *'spiritual'* Israel - i.e. the Church. *Codex Justinianus, 529AD – included legislation about religion. Numerous provisions serve to secure the status of Orthodox Christianity as the state religion of the empire, uniting Church and state, and making anyone who was not connected to the Christian church a non-citizen. (Wikipedia.org/Corpus_Juris_Civilis).

Many of the early Church Fathers were anti-Semites

The Church fathers were immediately faced with the problem of making their theory fit with literally hundreds, if not thousands, of prophecies and inspired statements in the Bible that refer to the ultimate *"Restoration of Israel"*. Even though the contexts in which many of these inspired statements are set clearly indicate reference to a *'literal'* and *'physical'* restoration of the Whole House of Israel, they attempted to rationalize this by *'spiritualizing'* them away. The Torah is primarily designed as a way of life. The influence of Hellenism i.e. Greek thinking became a major cause for anti-Semitism in the Christian church. Many of the early church fathers were very anti-Semitic in their thinking. By way of illustration, just look at a few of their comments:

Justin Martyr (100-165AD) claimed that God's covenant with the Jews was no longer valid and that the Gentiles had replaced the Jews in God's redemptive plan.

Ignatius (Bishop of Antioch in early 2nd century), wrote that anyone who celebrated Passover with the Jews, or received emblems of the Jewish feasts, was a partaker of those who killed the Lord and His Apostles.

Tertulian (one of the most influential writers of the second century), in his "Against the Jews" treatise blamed the entire Jewish race for the death of Jesus Christ.

Origen (185-253AD), accused the Jews of plotting to kill Christians. Origen was the one who introduced the allegorical interpretation of the Bible, where anything that spoke of a literal kingdom of Israel established here on the earth was seen as allegorical and spiritualized away. He taught that in the Scriptures the curses applied to the Jews, whereas the blessings applied to the Church, which was the 'new' Israel of God that had 'replaced' the literal Israel in the plan of God.

Eusebius (263-339AD), taught that the promises and blessings of the Bible were for the Christians and that the curses were for the Jews. Like the others he declared that the Church was the true Israel of God that had 'replaced' the literal Israel in God's covenants.

John Crysostom ((344-407AD) was yet another bishop at Antioch, and the greatest preacher of his day. His oratorical skills were such that he was known as "Golden Mouth". He said that there could never be forgiveness for the Jews and that God had always hated them. He taught that it was the 'Christian's duty' to hate the Jews. According to Crysostom the Jews were the assasins of Christ and worshippers of the devil.

Augustine (345-430AD) taught that the kingdom of God was not literal but spiritual. He taught the kingdom was present, not future and existed only in the hearts of men.

If you accept Augustine's writing, and the writings of the other chuch fathers, you, like millions of Christians around the world, believe that you are now living in the millennial kingdom of God on earth, which is the Church. Furthermore, many of you also believe that you are already living as a citizen of the New Jerusalem, which is spiritual. You also believe, despite all the evidence to the contrary, that the devil is effectively bound, and that the mother church is establishing God's rule over the earth. For centuries the Church has tried to impose its own interpretation on Scripture. The Bible, however, is a book about Israel, and Israel alone! Its entire text revolves around the covenant the LORD GOD (YHVH), the Holy One of Israel, made with a specific people and nation. This immutable and eternal covenant involved the promise of actual land here on the earth, i.e. the Promised Land.

The Oldest Title Deed on the Earth!

What the world fails to recognise, is that the Title Deed to the Holy Land is written down and recorded for all posterity in the Holy Bible. This book predates the Koran by a thousand years and is revered by Jews and Christians alike. It is written down in unambiguous language, giving clear boundaries and jurisdictions for the land. It is the oldest title deed in the world, which states unequivocally that the land belongs to Israel.

"And the LORD said to Abram: "Lift your eyes now and look from the place where you are – northward, southward, eastward, and westward; **"for all the land which you see I give to you and your descendants *forever.*** *"And I will make your descendants as the dust of the earth; so that if a man could number the dust of the earth, then your descendants also could be numbered.* **Arise, walk in the land through its length and its width, for I give it to you.** *" Then Abram moved his tent, and went and dwelt by the terebinth (oak) trees of Mamre, which are in* **Hebron**, *and built an altar there to the LORD."* (Genesis 13:14-18, editor's emphasis).

There is no other nation on the face of the earth that can remotely match the claim Israel has to their Land of Promise. No other nation can justify the claim to their land the way Israel can, through an Everlasting Divine Covenant. There is no clan, no tribe, or people on our planet who posses a written title deed to their land that is written by the hand of GOD.

On the same day the LORD made a covenant with Abram, saying: "To your descendants I have given this land, from the river of Egypt (the Nile) to the great river, the River Euphrates." (Genesis 15:18, NKJV).

"And I will establish My covenant between Me and you and your descendants after you in their generations, for **an everlasting covenant**, *to be God to you and your descendants after you. "Also I give to you and your descendants after you the land in which you are a stranger, all the land of Canaan, as an everlasting possession; and I will be their God."* (Genesis 17:7-8, NKJV, editor's emphasis).

GOD Himself deeded this land to His people Israel by an eternal covenant, which cannot be broken. The book also tells us who Israel is. Israel is composed of the descendants of the twelve sons of Jacob, the descendant of Abraham and Isaac, whose name was changed to Israel (Genesis 32:27-28). This makes the claim of the Palestinians totally irrelevant. It also exposes the spurious claims of Islam as false. The truth is that no power on earth can change the irrevocable WORD of YHVH, the Holy One of Israel, the Almighty Creator of the Universe and Ruler over All things.

The Hellenistic roots of Replacement Theology

One of the best expressions of this *'Replacement Theology'* is made by Dr. Robert Reymond, a highly respected systematic theologian from the United States in his article featured in the *"Sword and Trowel"* publication. He writes as follows:

'All God's land promises to Israel in the Old Testament are to be seen in terms of shadows, type and prophecy, in contrast to the reality, substance and fulfillment of which the New Testament speaks'.' We Christians, as members of Christ's Messianic Kingdom, we are the real heirs to the land promises of Holy scripture, but in their fulfilled character in the heavenly hereafter'.

The mindset of the Church has been conditioned by a Greek/Hellenistic mindset, a tendency that was intensified by the 'so called' Enlightenment with its preference for the abstract over against the particular. Yet, the books of the Bible are uniquely concrete and historical. The problem with this reasoning is that it tends to view the God of the Old Testament as being somehow different from the God of the New Testament. In some three thousand instances in the Hebrew Scriptures, and a further fourteen hundred instances in the apostolic writing that we refer to as the New Testament, the word 'God' is used, but always it is a reference to a particular God: **the God of Abraham, Isaac and Jacob.** The problem is that Christians tend to read the Bible from a Greek point of view, and consequently they lose sight of the fact that the Scriptures in both the Old and the New/ Renewed Testament refer to the God of Israel, *WHO IS THE SAME YESTERDAY, TODAY AND TOMMORROW.*

The Apostle Paul preached the Gospel of God!

The Apostle Paul did not have this problem, even though in his day, the spirit of Hellenism was the predominant influence amongst the ruling elites, as he approached the Gospel with a Hebrew mindset. We find evidence of this in his first words to the church at Rome:

"Paul, a bondservant of Jesus Christ, called to be an apostle, separated to THE GOSPEL OF GOD." (Romans 1:1, NKJV, emphasis added).

Paul here is speaking about the Hebrew God of Abraham, Isaac and Jacob, yet Christians just do not think that way. For Christians it is either *'The Gospel'*...period! Maybe they might express it as, *'the Gospel of Christ'*, or *'Christ's Gospel of the Kingdom'*. Yet, Paul speaking from a Hebrew perspective says it is the *"Gospel of God"*. He goes on to use the same phrase in the fifteenth chapter:

"Nevertheless, brethren, I have written more boldly to you on some points, as reminding you, because of the grace given to me by God, that I might be a minister of Jesus Christ to the Gentiles (former members of the lost house of Israel), ministering THE GOSPEL OF GOD, that the offering of the Gentiles might be acceptable, sanctified by the Holy Spirit" (Romans 15:15-16, NKJV, comments added).

In his first letter to the Thessalonians Paul uses the same terminology three times: *the Gospel of God!* The calling of the Apostle Paul is to proclaim the *'Good News'*, the *'Good News regarding God'*. For him this definition means, *'the God of Israel'*.

With all due respect, in the author's opinion, Christianity needs to understand that the *God of Israel*, the God of Abraham, Isaac and Jacob, has acted in Yeshua the Messiah for the sake of His lost sheep of the house of Israel. This is the God to whom Yeshua prayed. This is the God He served, and this is the God who raised our Savior from the dead. Christians tend to say *'Christ rose from the dead'*, but the

Scriptures attest again and again to the fact that God, the God of Israel, raised Yeshua from the dead.

When Yeshua directed His disciples in prayer, He directed their prayer to the Father, to the God of Abraham, Isaac and Jacob. He says, *"I have come to reveal the Father...for nobody knows the father like a son"*. Christianity has been conditioned through the centuries, with a Hellenistic philosophy, which has lost sight of the specific and true identity of God. This God even reveals His proper Name to Moses, a name by which He is remembered through all generations. Unfortunately in Christian tradition the name became distorted as 'Jehovah'. But His Name is YHVH. In Jewish tradition it is read as Adonai, and it is translated as the LORD in the King James Bible. It is by this Name YHVH, that He is named some three thousand times in the Hebrew Bible. This is the God who proclaims Himself as the God of Israel! He has a Name! He has an identity! In His sovereign Will He has graciously elected to choose a people and a nation – Israel – that through the family of Israel all the nations of the earth may be blessed.

The Big Story of the Bible is all about God!

Replacement Theology, or Supersessionism, as it is also called, first began in the second century. It held that the real story of the Bible from beginning to the end is all about redemption. The Church fathers in effect said: If you want to know the *"big story,"* start your search with Genesis chapters 1, 2 and 3 – the Creation and the Fall of mankind – then leapfrog all the way over to Matthew's Gospel and the birth of the Redeemer. Thus you have the Creation, you have the Fall of man, you have Redemption, and eventually you will have the Consummation in the *'heavenly'* Jerusalem. This is the classic narrative pattern of Scripture as read by the Church for twenty centuries in which God is viewed primarily as Creator and Redeemer.

Now is this true? Well, on the one hand, yes, it is true. God is a redeemer! But it is not the whole story, as when we look at the Bible with Hebraic eyes, there is an even bigger story going on in Scripture. Whereas the books of Exodus, Leviticus and Numbers speak about redemption, they are flanked on either side by Genesis and Deuteronomy, which speak of Covenant and Blessing.

Yet, in the Church's standard *'replacement'* model, most of the Hebrew Bible is considered irrelevant to the formulation of the Church's basic theology. All that is needed are the first three chapters of Genesis, the Gospels and the apostolic writings of the New Testament. Everything else is only useful for illustration and spiritual edification, but it has nothing decisive to say about God's story on the earth. They thus miss the fact that the big story is all about God. It is not about the Church, nor about you and me. In fact it is not even about Israel! It is about the GOD who sovereignly elected and chose to identify Himself with a family: Abraham and his descendants.

When it comes to telling the story of redemption from a Christian viewpoint, the story is usually related without any reference whatsoever to the God of Israel! All we have to say is: *"The God who created the universe was offended by man in his rebellion; but then, in His love rather than in His judgment, God sent a Redeemer, Jesus Christ, and now all who call upon the name of Jesus shall be saved, i.e. inherit a place in the world to come".*

Do we realize that the core of this story is told without any reference to the God of Abraham, Isaac and Jacob? And yet if we look at Genesis, we have three chapters devoted to Creation and the Fall of mankind, but we have thirty eight chapters devoted to the story of Abraham and his family! Viewed from a Hebraic perspective the first eleven chapters of Genesis are but a prelude to the place where the "big story" actually begins in Genesis 12, when God sovereignly elects Abraham and enters into covenant with him and his descendants. He says:

"I will make you a great nation; I will bless you and make your name great; and you shall be a blessing. I will bless those who bless you, and I will curse him who curses you; and in you all the Families of the earth shall be blessed." (Genesis 12:2-3, NKJV).

Blessing is a theme that runs from the beginning to the end of the Scriptures. It is integral even to the creation itself, the climax of the blessing being given on the Sabbath, the seventh day. It is the essence of God's dealing with Abraham and his descendants, the children of Israel. When He covenants with Abraham, it is not just to deal with sin, evil and wickedness in the world. Instead the covenant is defined as the means for blessing!

Thus the big story is that The LORD (YHVH) is a Creator, who wants to bless, and in order to achieve this goal, He covenants with a people to bring about the good that He intends, so that He may ultimately consummate, that is *'become at one'* with His creation.

The hidden irony in Christian Replacement Theology

The reason why Christianity has largely ignored the prophecies about the lost House of Israel is because of the replacement theology paradigm that has blinded their minds to the truth. The fact remains, that even if the Church at large were to miraculously accept the truth, it would contradict the established theology. While Christians have a concept of *'personal redemption'*, the *'national redemption'* the prophets of the Bible speak off, is something that is totally foreign to them. Nevertheless, nearly ninety percent of the prophetic books of the Bible are concerned about the *'national' redemption* of the House/Nation of Israel. The truth is that if the established Christian Church today were to recognize that all these prophecies refer to a *'literal'* and *'physical'* Israel after all, her entire theological card house would collapse. With this crucial vested interest at stake, it should not surprise us that their leaders are wholly opposed to any idea of a physical, literal Israel playing any role in end-time eschatology.

Nevertheless, there is a great deal of irony attached to this 'Christian' doctrine of 'Replacement Theology', as by usurping the position of the Covenant people of Israel, they are unwittingly associating themselves with the ancient Hebrews.

Whereas the original impetus for their replacement teaching was to steal the spiritual clothes of the Jews, they have in practice paid them a backhanded compliment! The early proponents of this Replacement Theology clearly thought that Israel's spiritual heritage was well worth stealing!

The point here is that people often tend to believe instinctively in something that they feel to be true, no matter how irrational. Their heart tells them that Israel's covenant heritage belongs to them, yet they cannot justify their entitlement with their head. It is something that they intuitively feel in their subconscious mind. Intuition has frequently served as a powerful tool for discovery and invention, and many scientific and other research breakthroughs have their origin in just such intuitive feelings.

Why do Christians want to steal the clothes of the Jews?

The question is why does Christianity want to equate itself with Israel? Why do Christians want to make that connection?

Could it possibly be that, despite this widespread theory, the Christian Church has replaced Israel in God's scheme of things, that in this we are in fact seeing a further subliminal indicator of the Israelite origins of many of its believers? Might it be that it is a question of their own hidden Hebrew roots somehow telling them that they are entitled to Israel's heritage?

As we ponder this question, we may be uncovering a truth that has lain dormant inside the Christian breast for nearly two millennia. This means that in embracing this pernicious anti-Semitic *'replacement theology,'* Christians may actually unwittingly be revealing their own Israelite origins as the Lost Tribes of Israel. They subconsciously desire to equate themselves as Israel because; if the truth be known, they are Israel! Is this not highly ironic? They don't know it and if you told them they would deny it! Yet, deep inside buried in their DNA they somehow sense the Israel calling belongs to them. This means that even this adherence by the Church to *'replacement theology'* might well be a further *'sign'* confirming the Hebrew roots of Christianity at large.

Athens versus Jerusalem

The problem with modern materialistic thought is that it is based entirely upon Hellenistic or Greek philosophy. The Greeks had difficulty relating the physical to the spiritual. This spirit of Hellenism influenced the minds of the Church fathers via the great schools of learning of the day, which were steeped in the theories of Plato and the other Greek philosophers.

Even as we observe society today, we see the west living in materialism, whereas the east dwells in a world of mysticism. In between these two worlds we find the ancient civilization of the Hebrews straddling the centre, living between east and west.

Yet, to the Hebrew mindset, both the physical and the spiritual are two sides of the same coin, with the physical being a type of the spiritual and *vice versa*. The fact is that Western thought has been influenced far more by Greek philosophy than by Hebrew theology. It is true to say that much of the world has failed to see the close connection between the physical and the spiritual.

A learned Jewish sage once describes this totally different mindset between the Greeks and the Hebrews in a most poetic way. He stated that the Athenian Greeks in their philosophy made the mistake of separating the heart from the head. This is a highly unbalanced theory, as is plain for all to see, that the head cannot do without the heart, and neither can the heart function without the head. Most of us know only too well that the heart has its own way of knowing and so does the head, and neither should be ignored. It is not unusual for people sometimes to instinctively believe in something that they feel to be true but cannot prove. Their heart tells them that something is true, yet they cannot square it with their head. It is something they feel intuitively. This lies at the root of the Christian belief in their entitlement to the covenant promises made to the patriarchs of Israel.

The truth is that the philosophies of our western society are underpinned by the belief systems of only two ancient cities, Athens and Jerusalem. Athens represents human reason based upon observation of the five senses through experimentation and measurement. For this reason Athens will always fall short, as it is limited entirely to the physical realm. Jerusalem on the other hand represents a higher dimension, containing abstract spiritual concepts and realities such as sacrifice, freedom, love, faith and hope.

Whereas man's head may come from Athens, it is in Jerusalem where his heart is found. Athens is a faithless city where there is no hope, while true faith is found in Jerusalem. Without faith a man is as good as dead. Faith is more powerful than science, just as the heart is stronger than the head. Faith should never be relegated to something that is inferior to science, as it is in faith that vision resides, and without vision the people perish.

The establishment of the State of Israel changed everything!

The sudden arrival on the world scene of the Jewish State of Israel served as a mighty 'wake up' call for many pastors and believers inside the Church. The event drew many to re-examine their beliefs in the light of the prophesies of the Bible, which had found their dramatic fulfillment in the miraculous re-establishment of the Jewish State in its original location. They noted how the prophet Isaiah had prophesied the rebirth of the State of Israel some 2,700 years ago, when he pronounced the following:

"Who has heard such a thing? Who has seen such things? Shall the earth be made to give birth in one day? Or shall a nation be born at once? For as soon as Zion was in labor, she gave birth to her children" (Isaiah 66:8, NKJV).

This prophecy was fulfilled exactly as stated, when on May 14, 1948, *'in one day'* the State of Israel came into being. What the world fails to recognise is that the establishment of the State of Israel is in accordance with God's plan and purpose. His Divine plan is to ultimately restore the Davidic Kingdom and reunite the Two Houses of Israel. The re-establishment of the State of Israel in 1948 is one of the greatest political miracles in the history of the world, and this fact alone signifies that we live at the dawn of the glorious Messianic Age to come.

Never before in the annals of mankind has a universally despised people, who some two thousand years ago were expelled from their territory, only to be scattered to the four corners of the earth, succeeded in maintaining their identity for circa twenty centuries, for them to subsequently re-establish their nation in their original homeland! Yet, the prophets of the Bible have made specific promises to that end. The establishment of the State of Israel in 1948, was in effect a Biblical SIGN of super importance, to show the world that the 'time of the end' had begun. This was then followed by the rapid fulfilment of a whole series of prophesies, leading up to the forecast that in due course of time Israel will be hated by the whole world, culminating in a last global attempt to extinguish the Jewish race.

Partial Christian repentance

Thus when the Jews, after nearly 2,000 years of exile, re-established an independent state in Palestine in 1948, in direct fulfillment of hundreds of Bible prophecies, it did produce a startling shock to some Christian churches. This was especially so in the smaller Protestant evangelical denominations. Then, when the Jews in the Six Day War of 1967 routed their Arab enemies and conquered East Jerusalem, thus bringing their sacred capital once again under Jewish control, it provided a further jolt to Christian thinking. The result was that some in the Protestant wing of the Christian Church started to reject 'Replacement Theology', as they began to rethink their doctrines and beliefs about Israel. They began to acknowledge that God had a divine purpose for Israel (the Jewish nation), as well as for the Church. They came to see 'Replacement Theology' as a Christian form of anti-Semitism, and began to preach against it by advocating Christian repentance. Their campaign met with considerable success. This was especially the case in Protestant Evangelical; Pentecostal and Charismatic circles in the United States and England.

The last 30 years have seen a dramatic change in Christian attitudes towards Israel, with multiple scores of Christian organizations around the world heavily emphasizing the special importance of Israel and the Jewish people. In direct consequence, Christian Zionism has experienced a major resurgence especially in the English speaking world. Another more recent phenomenon is the worldwide growth of the Hebrew Roots movement with literally millions of Christians being drawn to observing the Torah. Many of these even feel inexorably drawn to return to the Land of Israel, which they believe to be the Land of their patriarchal Fathers. In this we have yet another indicator that something very big is afoot. This awakening of many Christians to their Hebrew roots is a sign that we truly live in the age of Messiah, and that the reunification of the Two Houses of Israel cannot now be too far away! Worldwide some sixty million Christians are unreservedly standing with Israel against the rising global tide of virulent hatred coming especially from the world of Islam. The encouraging news is that the numbers of Christian supporters of the Jewish State of Israel are growing day by day.

CHAPTER TEN

HOW DID IT ALL GO WRONG?

Scriptural love is predicated upon obedience

In western thought, the 'heart' is seen as the seat of the emotions and this is especially true of love. Yet, scriptural love is not an emotion, but an action of obedience. It is important to realise that in Hebraic thought, the heart is the seat of the MIND, INTELLECT and WILL. This Hebraic way of thinking is deeply imbedded in both the Old and the Renewed Testament writings. Due to the overwhelming influence of Hellenism in western education today, this is often misunderstood. Good intentions alone are not enough! YHVH, Our Father, demands our obedience, as obedience is the action that should flow from our love for Him. The Apostle James describes it as follows:

"But be doers of the word, and not hearers only, deceiving yourselves." (James 1:22).

"But he who looks into the perfect LAW OF LIBERTY and continues in it, and is not a forgetful hearer but a doer of the work, this one will be BLESSED in what he does". (James 1:25, NKJV, emphasis added).

Notice that the first five Books of Moses are being referred to here as the *'Law of Liberty'!*

Liberty is the exact opposite of bondage and slavery, and the one who is willing to observe this Law/instruction, and put it into practice in his life, will be *'blessed'* in what he does. Thus the *'instructions'* of our Heavenly Father, when obeyed, are designed to bring forth blessings upon us.

This is the kind of love our Heavenly Father expects from us His *'chosen'* people. Remember, we are NOT speaking of an emotional feeling, but of what the Bible defines as love. It is His definition of love which is required of us all. Remember, the words of Yeshua? He said: *"If you love Me keep My commandments!"* Sadly, such is the strength of the western and indeed Christian paradigm of 'love', that only the few will grasp the true meaning. The prophet Hosea, speaking of the rebellious children of Israel in his day said:

"My people are destroyed for lack of knowledge. Because you have rejected knowledge, I also will reject you from being a priest for Me; Because you have forgotten the law of your God, I will also forget your children". (Hosea 4:6, NKJV).

The heart is the Hebraic seat of the MIND, and of KNOWLEDGE, from which springs our love through obedience to His *Law of Liberty.* Good intentions are not good enough, and, as the Scripture says, without knowledge people are destroyed.

The Bible shows that good intentions alone will not do!

The nation of Israel worshipped golden calves with the 'best' of intentions. What??? That's idolatry! How can idolatry be done with good intentions? In Exodus 32 we find the account of the golden calf at Sinai. What is often missed in reading this account is that the children of Israel were not worshipping a different God. They were still worshipping the God (Elohim) of Israel, but they were doing it in a way He forbade. In verse one the people ask Aaron to make an Elohim to go before them. Aaron obliges and meets their request. Then in verse four they declare what this golden calf is: *"This is your god, O Israel, that brought you out of the land of Egypt!"*

This all took place whilst the smoke and fire of YHVH's Shekinah Glory was STILL on Mount Sinai where they were. They certainly were not trying to compete with the awesome Elohim (God) of Israel, by introducing another deity. If that is not clear enough, then look at verse 5. Aaron builds an altar in front of it and declares: *"Tomorrow is a feast to YHVH."* He did not declare a feast to the calf, but to the Elohim of Israel.

The Israelites were not 'replacing' the LORD GOD (YHVH), they were replacing Moses who had not returned for nearly forty days. They were substituting the mediator and physical symbol they followed. They believed with the best of intentions they were still following YHVH, the Holy One of Israel. Of course, the problem was that this was NOT how He had commanded worship. Their good intentions simply were not enough, as they soon found out when Moses returned from the mountain.

The Church is walking in the footsteps of King Jeroboam

Another example is found when the northern kingdom separated from the house of David in the south. The account is related in 1 Kings 12. Where we find king Jeroboam setting up golden calves in the cities of Bethel and Dan! Yet again, those worshiping there had good intentions and thought they were worshipping YHVH, the Holy One of Israel. Why did they do it? We find the reason was political, as is shown by the context:

And Jeroboam said in his heart, "Now the kingdom may return to the house of David: "If these people go up to offer sacrifices in the house of the Lord at Jerusalem, then the heart of this people will turn back to their lord, Rehoboam king of Judah." (1 Kings 12:26-27, NKJV).

Clearly, it was a political decision, as king Jeroboam was afraid that if his people continued their lifelong practice of going to worship at Solomon's Temple in Jerusalem, they might come under the influence of the king of Judah. In order to preserve his own dynasty, this is the one thing he wanted to prevent. Hense king Jeroboam made the following decision:

Therefore the king asked advice, made two calves of gold, and said to the people, "It is too much for you to go up to Jerusalem. Here are your gods, O Israel, which brought you up from the land of Egypt!" (1 Kings 12:28, NKJV).

Notice, that Jeroboam is substituting those golden calves as symbols, and he identifies them as representing YHVH, the Elohim of Israel, who brought them out of Egypt! He was thus directing sacrifice to YHVH at these new places for worship. At the root of Jeroboam's decision was a lack of trust. All of this could have avoided if the king had followed the advice of King Solomon in the book of Proverbs:

"Trust in the LORD with all your heart, and lean not unto your own understanding; In all your ways acknowledge Him, and He shall direct your paths."
(Proverbs 3:5-6, NKJV).

Trusting with the 'heart' is trusting with the MIND, not with the emotions, as your emotions will frequently deceive you. It is not about blind faith, but all about knowledge – His knowledge, as expounded in the first five books of Moses, i.e. the foundation of all of the Scriptures. Jeroboam ignored this. He even appointed non Levitical priests, and changed the times and the seasons, by creating his own holy days set apart for worship, (1Kings 12:33). The new feast he ordained; *"in the month which he had devised in his own heart"*. Thus the Scripture makes it absolutely clear that this was not from YHVH, and that this was in effect a blatant departure from His commandments.

If Jeroboam had relied on the mind of Our Father in Heaven, and acted according to His clearly laid down instructions, much grief would have been avoided. Today, the Christian descendants of those Israelites suffer from having made the same bad choice. The Bible in which the Holy One of Israel, has shown His *'chosen'* people how to live by His standards, is still present in every Christian home. The truth is that obedience has its own reward, as all those who are willing to live that way are set to inherit a multitude of blessings. God, the Elohim of Israel, asked His people to worship Him on the Sabbath, the seventh day of the week. He also commanded them to observe His appointed times, as He said to His people: *"These are My feasts!"* Yet, Christianity today is walking in the footsteps of Jeroboam, as it too has come up with an alternative to the commandments. In their own hearts they have devised Sunday worship and instituted Christmans and Easter, all of which, as is well known, are pagan in origin.

All along, they claim to love Him and follow Him with the very best of intentions, but in reality they worship Him after the same manner as those worshipping the golden calf. *"No, really, it's OK, our leaders said it was OK, we can worship this way now, as the LORD sees our hearts".*

Yes, He does see the heart! He sees a mind rejecting His commandments. He sees His people doing things their own way rather than His way. At Sinai, over three thousand men paid the price for that assumption with their lives. When it was repeated by Jeroboam, it started a chain of wilful disobedience which would end with the ten tribes being disowned from the Covenant! It took the death of Yeshua, the Son of the Highest, to enable them to be restored to a Renewed Covenant. How many will needlessly perish today, thinking they *'love'* Him. How many in this end-time will heed the words of Yeshua in His sermon on the mount? Yeshua, was speaking to all of His people when He said:

"Not everyone who says to Me, 'Lord, Lord', shall enter the kingdom of heaven, but HE WHO DOES THE WILL OF MY FATHER in heaven. "Many will say to Me in that day, 'Lord, Lord, have we not prophesied in Your name, cast out demons in Your name, and done many wonders in Your name?' "And then I will declare to them, 'I NEVER KNEW YOU; DEPART FROM ME, YOU WHO PRACTICE LAWLESSNESS!" (Matthew 7:21-23, NKJV, emphasis added).

Are these not the most terrible words any Christian believer would ever want to hear? They must surely rank as the most sobering words in the whole Bible. Is it not extraordinary that you can be a believer in Yeshua, and accept Him as your personal Savior, and yet fail in His eyes? You may even have prophesied in His name, cast out demons in

His name and done many wonders in His name and still be rejected by Him. Can you believe it? This is serious!

Notice, Yeshua says that MANY of His followers will be rejected by Him, and refused entry into His kingdom, for practicing lawlessness! What might He possibly mean? It does not take a genius to work out that He is referring to the Law of His Father. He is addressing those who, much like their ancient Hebrew ancestors before them, choose not to obey the Fathers commandments, but rather make up rules they have devised in their own hearts. In others words, whatever the law may be, they prefer not to obey it.

You are not under the Law but under Grace?

In the Garden of Eden, Adam and Eve were being offered a simple choice by their Creator. The choice was between the Tree of Life and the Tree of the Knowledge of Good and Evil. These trees were symbolic of two ways of life that were completely opposed to eachother. They were instructed that they could eat of every tree in the garden and this included the fruit of the Tree of Life. Had they chosen to eat of this tree it would have brought them untold physical as well as spiritual blessings. The Tree of Life, as the name implies, would have given them eternal life.

YHVH, the Creator had clearly spelled out the consequences for making the wrong choice. Both Adam and Eve knew full well that if they ate of the Tree of the Knowledge of Good and Evil, that they would surely die. They knew that one choice meant life eternal and that the other meant death. It was made very clear to them. We all know the story of what choice they made. They made the same choice that every man, woman or child has made ever since. They wanted to do it their way! It is natural for man to always want to do this. It is the human condition, and it is commonly referred to as human nature. Humans naturally do not want to walk in the paths of righteousness. We all know this from our own experience, as well as from the experience of our children. Yes, we see this same spirit of rebellion and wilful stubbornness even in the baby years of our children. The choice of the Tree of Life versus the Tree of Knowledge has never gone away. Even Moses, when exhorting the children of Israel, to keep the commandments of God, the Elohim of Israel, knew full well that they would fail. In his final testament to the twelve tribes of Israel, he placed before them the same choice the Creator and the Father of Israel, had placed before Adam and Eve.

"I call heaven and earth as witnesses today against you, that I have set before you life and death, blessing and cursing; therefore choose life, that both you and your descendants may live." (Deuteronomy 30:19, NKJV).

The whole story of the Old Testament is the account of how the Israelites failed time and again to stay on the right course. The world at large has failed to choose 'life' in an even bigger way. It is true to say that, once we start to measure ourselves by God's own standards, the whole world has failed and man is an abject failure before Elohim. The Apostle Paul pointed out that: *"we would not have known sin except through the law."*

The inference in this is that the Law (Torah) came into play to 'highlight' the sinfulness of breaking the commandments. It was introduced to mankind that they do not measure up to God's divine standards. Yet, the Law was also introduced to show man how they might enjoy an abundant life filled with true happiness and blessings, if they would only choose to submit and obey. The Law is the yardstick by which we can measure our life against the standards of Our Father in Heaven. Thus the Law is the gauge by which we can measure the sinfulness of our character. This is what the apostle Paul instructed his followers to do:

"Therefore do not let sin reign in your mortal body, that you should obey its lusts."
(Romans 6:12, NKJV).

Paul says that we must not allow sin to rule in our bodies. Sin, as the Apostle John puts it is: *"the transgression of the law!"* (1John 3:4) Paul is definitely not saying that we should get rid of the law and make out that it does not apply anymore. He is saying exactly the opposite! Paul says here that we must not allow sin, or the transgression of the Law, to rule in our mortal bodies, so that it makes you obey its desires. He then goes on to point out the reason by saying:

"For sin shall not have dominion over you, for you are not under the law (legalism) but under grace." (Romans 6:14, NKJV, comment added).

Now why is Paul saying to the disciples that they are not under the Law? We need to understand the background Paul came from. He was brought up in Torah. He was an eminent scholar and a pupil of the great Gamaliel. He was a Rabbi and a teacher of the Law. All of a sudden he says that we are not under the Law, but that we are under grace. What does he mean? The distinction is quite simple really. Paul has become aware that humanly none of us is keeping the Law. Man is simply incapable of obeying the just requirements of God's perfect Law. No human being can possibly live up to the perfect standards of our Creator. We are totally inadequate within ourselves to obey the just demands of the Torah. **That means we are under the Law!** You are under it! You, just like all the other lost sheep of the house of Israel, are under its curse. You are under its oppression and you are under its penalty. The law has become much like the 'Sword of Damocles' hanging over you. If you are going through the motions of keeping the law, knowing full well that you are certain to fall short, then it becomes mere legalism. If you are living by a set of rules that you cannot abide by, the consequences of your failure will hang over you, because you know there really is no solution. Paul, as a Torah observant rabbi had experienced this. He had all his life with all his heart and with all his might tried to obey the Torah, and yet he had failed to keep the spiritual intent behind the Torah, which His Master, Messiah Yeshua, had come to reveal. He knew the Torah by heart and yet he had failed to keep it to the standards that YHVH in His perfect righteousness demanded. As a Jew and as a rabbi, he had enjoyed every advantage and yet he failed. He was one of those rare people who could see the equation. He could understand how something as beautiful and perfect as the Torah could become a threat to you. He could understand how it could become oppression to you, as no one is able to keep the just requirements of YHVH's holy, righteous and spiritual law. Thus, something that should be your friend has become something that would condemn you. That is the reason why the apostle says: *"You are not under the law but you are under grace."*

What does Grace mean?

Literally it means 'unmerited pardon'. The spiritual meaning refers to our condition. If you are 'under grace' you have been empowered by the Holy Spirit (the Spirit of YHVH) inside of you to attain unto salvation and eternal life. That is the 'grace' you have received, because, as an incorrigible and habitual sinner, you did not deserve it. You came into the sacrifice of Yeshua (Jesus), who died on your behalf, and who paid the penalty for your sins. He also paid the price for Adam's failure to make the right choice in the first place. Thus, by accepting Yeshua, as your personal Savior, you came into a condition of 'grace', which you did not derserve, because, as a serial sinner, all you deserve is death!

The Scripture makes it quite clear that this is what we all deserve; *"as there is none righteous no not one!"* Having received the gift of the Holy Spirit, you have now obtained the power to impart within you the righteousness of YHVH, which enables you to fulfil the just requirements of His law. This means that you no longer have to live 'UNDER', it but instead you can live 'IN' it. That is the difference! **Grace enables you to live within the law!**

It is because of that same 'grace' that you come to love the law and the commandments of Elohim. You are able to live 'within' the law, as the Spirit of Elohim within you enables you, not only to keep the law, but also to fulfil the spiritual intent behind the law. Thus it is indeed 'BY GRACE' that the true disciple of Messiah Yeshua, is able to walk, as He walked, in perfect obedience to the law of His Father. This is not legalism! This is nothing other than a demonstration of true love. Remember, those immortal words of Yeshua: *"If you love Me, keep My commandments"*. The Apostle John points out something about the commandments that is most frequently overlooked by believers:

"By this we know that we love the children of God (children of Israel), when we love God, and keep his commandments. For this is the love of God, that we keep his commandments: and HIS COMMANDMENTS ARE NOT GRIEVOUS".
(1John 5:2-3, KJV, comment & emphasis added).

Mankind needs to understand that the commandments are not given to hurt or to restrict us, but that the sole purpose behind the the establishment of the Law by a loving Elohim, is to direct man into a path that will produce perfect peace of mind, happiness and an abundant life of blessings. Once we are empowered by the Spirit of YHVH within us, our minds are transformed, and we want to keep His commandments simply because we love Him. You do not do it out of fear, or because you feel you have to. We do not do it out of a misguided belief that keeping the commandments is somehow going to earn you your salvation. Absolutely not! We are keeping the commandments of our Father in Heaven because we love Him. In our obedience we are also declaring our love for Yeshua, our Savior, Redeemer, Master and Lord, even as we walk in His footsteps. We obey Him because we love Him, and that is all there is to it!

How can you love Jesus and Hate the Law of His Father?

Yeshua said: *"I and My Father are one!"* Therefore for anyone professing to love Jesus, whilst at the same time hating the law of His Father, would almost certainly receive that awesome rebuke from Yeshua: *"I never knew you; depart from Me, you who practice lawlessness!"*

Satan is a lawbreaker and he hates the Law of God. He is the ultimate rebel and an archdeceiver. He hates anyone who who walks with YHVH, by observing His Law. Satan is the God of this world, and in this world, keeping the commandments is not a popular activity. Satan has distilled his spirit of rebellion into the world and the world hates the Law/ instructions of its Creator. The Apostle Paul makes this very clear:

"The carnal mind is enmity against God; for it is not subject to the law of God, nor indeed can be." (Romans 8:7, NKJV).

Can you see what the Apostle Paul is saying? He clearly explains that the carnal or fleshly natural mind of man hates God! WHY? Paul answers the question: *'Because it is not subject to the law of God!'* The reverse side of this equation is that, if only man would be subject to to God's law, man would love God. Can we see the connection?

The History of our Jewish brothers is a case in point. Satan's hatred for the law of God makes him hate every

Torah observant Jew. This is the root cause for the virulent disease known as anti-Semitism, which has a history going back four thousand years to the Pharaoh of Egypt. This is why the Jews throughout their history have always been persecuted by the world. It is because they, as the people of the Book of the Law, have been the odd ones out. They have always stood out like the proverbial sore thumb. Their insistence in keeping the commandments of YHVH, has been a continuing thorn in Satan's side, and this is why he has always wanted to wipe them out. In the past he has used the Christian church to great effect, as his instrument in being a special scourge to the Jews. The Church has persecuted them through murderous genocidal crusades, pogroms, inquisitions, and expulsions, as well as through the ultimate horrors of the Holocaust.

Today Satan is using Islam to try to root out the Jews and expunge them from the face of the earth, with much of the Christian Church choosing the side of their enemies. Tomorrow, Satan will use the EU, in unholy partnership with Islam, to annihilate the Jews, as well as those who dare to support them. Satan hates the Law of Elohim and he has instilled this same hatred into the hearts of men. The Church, in the formation of its doctrines, has been subject to the same influence. The remarkable fact is, that the Christian Church is split into a thousand or more denominations, who espouce many differing doctrines and articles of faith. They disagree among themselves on almost every subject or doctrine, yet when it comes of the law having been abolished, they speak with one voice! This fact alone should make one suspicious! What might be the reason for this extraordinary unity among all of those numerous Christian denominations? In this, their voice is none other than the voice of satan, the arch deceiver and the prince of rebellion, who hates the law of God! It is because of this hatred that the Church is saying that the Law is done away!

The Parable of the Wheat and the Tares

Most Christians are familiar with the parable of the wheat and the tares, which Yeshua used as an analogy of His kingdom. The account is about a man who sowed good quality seed in his field and late at night, whilst he was asleep, an enemy came and sowed bad seed, or tares in that same field. The enemy wanted to wreck the harvest, because he hated the owner of the field. When the grain appeared, the labourers noticed that the grain was almost smothered by the tares, or weeds. They questioned their master about the quality of the seed that he had sown, and they were told that an enemy had gone out of his way to deliberately spoil the harvest. The workmen then wanted to clear the field of those wretched tares that were so badly affecting the crop. However, their master told them to leave well alone until the time of the harvest. The owner of the field was concerned, that if the tares were pulled up at this stage, it might possibly damage his precious wheat. When the time of the harvest came, the reapers were told to first collect the tares in bundles ready for burning, and to then collect the wheat to be stored in the barn.

After Yeshua had relayed this parable to the multitude, His disciples asked Him privately, what message He was trying to get across to the people. They asked Him to explain the meaning of the parable. This is how Yeshua answered them:

He who sows the good seed is the Son of man. The field is the world, the good seeds are the sons of the kingdom, but the bad seeds are the sons of the wicked one. The enemy who sowed them is the devil, the harvest is the end of the age, and the reapers are the the angels". (Matthew 13:37-39, NKJV).

Here we have in a nutshell, yet another example of the Gospel of the Kingdom, which Yeshua had come to preach.

It is He who sows the good seed that leads to obedience, and conversely it is the devil, who sows the bad seed that leads to disobedience or lawlessness. Now let us see what happens to those lawless ones:

"The Son of man will send out His angels, and they will gather out of His kingdom all things that offend, and those who practice lawlessness, and will cast them into a furnace of fire. There will bewailing and gnashing of teeth." (Matthew 13:41-42, NKJV).

The Oxford English reference dictionary describes a tare as *'an injurious weed'* resembling wheat when young. A tare is thus described as a counterfeit of the real article. The word is apparently of Arabic origin and is derived from the word *'tarba'* which means *'reject'*. Here in this parable, Yeshua gives His disciples His own definition of what a tare truly is. To summarise His words: **"A tare is an offensive, good for nothing, and lawless weed that is only good for burning, and which will not be allowed to enter My Kingdom!"**

Notice also that, as His angels gather these lawless tares, they will wail and gnash their teeth in anger and utter frustration. Why, this extreme reaction? These lawless weeds had assumed that, all the time they were growing up in YHVH's field, they actually thought they were wheat! All their lives they thought THEY were the righteous ones. They thought that because they were 'SAVED by GRACE', they therefore did not have to keep the the law or the commandments. They thought the law had been done away with. They had assumed that it had been nailed to the cross. Yeshua concludes His parable with a final warning:

"He who has ears to hear, let him hear!"

Who are the Two Witnesses?

The word 'witness' in Hebrew is *'ed'*, it means witness, testimony and recorder. It comes from the root word *'ood'* meaning *to duplicate!* Thus the root of the word witness in Hebrew means to duplicate, just like a tape recorder, or camcorder duplicates everything that is said or seen. The Law of Witness was first established in the Ten Commandments (Exodus 20:16, and it is repeated again in Deuteronomy 5:20. It is clearly very important to YHVH, that no one should be judged or put to death on the testimony of just one witness. There had to be two, and if possible three witnesses to put someone to death. Very interesting! The question is who are these witnesses? When before any court a witness has to give his testimony and in this fact we are given the key to the answer, as we read:

"And Moses turned and went down from the mountain, and the TWO TABLETS OF TESTIMONY were in his hand. The tablets were written on both sides; on the one side and on the other they were written." (Exodus 32:15, NKJV, emphasis added).

Here we have authoritative confirmation that the two witnesses are those two tablets of stone upon which are written the Ten Commandments, they represent all of the Torah. The next question is, are there any more witnesses? Who else are established as His witnesses? Who else has YHVH declared as His witnesses on the earth? The Prophet Isaiah provides us with the answer:

"You are My witnesses", says the LORD, "And My servant whom I have chosen, that you may know and believe Me, and understand that I am He. Before Me there was no God formed, nor shall there be after Me." (Isaiah 43:10, NKJV).

In this chapter the prophet is addressing Israel, and notice, he uses the plural, *"You are My witnesses"*. This means that Israel, like those two tablets of stone, had to be composed of at least two witnesses! In Isaiah 44:8, the statement concerning Israel is repeated once again, and then we find Yeshua reiterating the same principle to His disciples, just prior to His ascension to heaven:

"But you shall receive power when the Holy Spirit has come upon you; and you shall be witnesses to Me in Jerusalem, and in all Judea and Samaria, and to the end of the earth". (Acts 1:8, NKJV).

The same two witnesses are also referred to in the book of Revelation:

"And I will give power to My two witnesses, and they will prophesy one thousand two hundred and sixty days, clothed in sackcloth." These are the two olive trees and the two lampstands standing before the God of the earth. (Revelation 11:3-4, NKJV).

Most Bible scholars have interpreted that to mean that at the end of the age these two witnesses will be testifying for three and a half years against the lawless forces of the anti-Christ, and that they are two individuals. Whereas, this may certainly be the case, there exixts yet another possibility, as evidenced by the two olive trees and the two lampstands referred to in verse four. Maybe, we should consider another possible scenario for the events described. Accepting that these two witnesses may well be two individual persons, the likelihood is that they will be backed up by substantial companies of people that will be testifying of the imminent arrival of the Kingdom of God. This is speaking of the the Two Houses of Israel, i.e. the Two Olive Trees, the olive tree being the symbol of Israel.

Now why have those two witnesses? Go back to the law of witness! It takes the testimony of at least two witnesses to put a person to death! What is coming after they witness to the earth for three and a half years? DIVINE JUDGMENT – how many witnesses does it take before the death penalty may be given? At least two! Remember, Isaiah has already made it clear that; *'all of Israel are to be His witnesses in the earth'*. This means that both houses of Israel, Judah and Ephraim are going to be YHVH's witnesses on the earth. The witness will be done by two companies, who represent the **two faces of Israel, Christians and Jews, i.e. Israel and Judah.** You see if we use just Ephraim/Israel as a witness, we do not have two witnesses. If we use just Judah as YHVH's witnesses in the earth, we still have only one witness. For the witness to be effective we need Christians and Jews to become one in Messiah, speeding the day for the reunification of the restored Kingdom of Israel.

The Wheat and the Tares revisited

In the book of Deuteronomy the Israelites are told not to sow different kinds of seed in the same field. (Deuteronomy 22:9). Thus in the Torah i.e the teaching of YHVH, we may not mix species of plants or seeds and you may not yoke two species of animals together. In the Hebrew Mishnah, this law is called the law of Kilayim, meaning the law of 'two kinds'. This law of kilayim also includes the prohibition of not grafting any two species together. This helps us to understand the Apostle Paul's comments on the subject of being grafted into the olive tree of Israel in Romans chapter eleven. You cannot take the branches of an apple tree and graft them into a cherry tree. You cannot take branches of a peach tree and graft them into a pear tree. It is forbidden by YHVH. You cannot do that because you are grafting two different species together. The Apostle Paul, one of the greatest Torah scholars who ever lived, brings up this same law of kilayim – the law of two kinds, and applies it to the elect believers in Messiah Yeshua. Notice, how Paul applies this law of two kinds:

"Do not be unequally yoked together with unbelievers. For what fellowship has righteousness with lawlessness? And what communion has light with darkness? And what accord has Christ with Belial? Or what part has a believer with an unbeliever? And what agreement has the temple of God with idols? For you are the temple of the living God. As God has said: "I will dwell in them and walk among them. I will be their God, and they shall be My people." Therefore "Come out from among them, and be separate, says the LORD. Do not touch what is unclean, and I will receive you." "I will be a Father to you and you shall be My sons and daughters, says the LORD Almighty". (2Corinthians 6:14-18, NKJV).

The Apostle Paul understood the principle behind the law of kilayin, because he knew that if a believer married an unbeliever it was an unequal yoke. The Torah teaches that if you yoke an ass with an ox, you have an unequal yoke, because the ass cannot keep up with the ox in the labor. It will literally die because the ox is a sturdier animal. So, it is also with humans, and when you come into an unholy mixture something has to give.

Now going back to the parable of the sower, what do we have sown in the field? We have two kinds of seed, one good and one bad! Did YHVH sow the bad seed? He says, *an enemy came and sowed this bad seed, in the wheat field.*

What does this wheat in the wheatfield imply? John the Baptist, in speaking about the one who would come after him, and whose sandals he was not worthy to carry, gives us the answer, as he said:

"His winnowing fan is in His hand, and He will thoroughly clean out His threshing floor, and gather His wheat into the barn; but He will burn up the chaff with unquencheable fire." (Matthew 3:12, NKJV).

The wheat spoken off here is symbolic of Israel. The wheat is Israel! Remember, Yeshua refers to the good seed in His parable as *the sons of the kingdom!* Which kingdom? It's the reunited and restored kingdom of Israel! Messiah Yeshua is going to gather His wheat i.e, the children of Israel, into His barn, but then there are some tares. *The angels will come and gather out of His kingdom all things that offend.* Did you notice that at the time of the harvest, the tares are to be bound up in bundles and burned? This is speaking of judgment at the end of the age! Those tares are variously referred to in the parable as the *'sons of the wicked one'* (verse 38), and as, *'those who practice lawlessness'* (verse 41). How can the 'wheat' be anything else but redeemed Israel, if we understand that lawlessness means anti-Torah teaching? As the Apostle Paul says: *"All Israel will be saved!"* (Romans 11:26). This is speaking of Christians and Jews alike, who together make up the two faces of Israel, as it is not just the Jews alone! Remember, there were twelve tribes who stood there at Mount Sinai when the Torah, the marriage covenant, was given.

How to provoke the Jew to jealousy?

The Apostle Paul in his famous letter to the community of believers at Rome, wrote about the two houses of Israel. He covered the subject extensively in three chapters of his letter to the Romans. There we find one key phrase which is often picked up and used by Christians, which states:

"I say then, have they stumbled that they should fall? Certainly not! But through their fall, to PROVOKE THEM TO JEALOUSY, salvation has come to the Gentiles." Romans 11:11. NKJV, emphasis added).

Those 'Gentiles' the apostle is speaking about are a reference to those, *'lost sheep of the house of Israel'* Yeshua had commissioned His disciples to find. (Matthew 10:6). Their commission was *to bring SALVATION to the Gentiles!* Earlier Yeshua, our Jewish Messiah had emphasised that, *SALVATION is of the Jews!* (John 4:22). He sent out His Jewish disciples to proclaim His name 'Yeshua', which equals 'Salvation', to the Gentile sons of Israel. Here the Apostle Paul is now urging those same Gentile sons of Israel to make their brother Judah jealous!

What will it take to make those of the house of Judah truly jealous of Christian members of the house of Israel? Judging by the lack of success of nearly two thousand years of evangelising, it surely cannot be the way the Christian Church has gone about presenting its message about Jesus Christ. Had that been the case, Judah would have been flocking to the Christian fold long ago.

Consider this, in the early first century body of Messiah, all the believers were Jewish and came from Judah, or close to Judah. Great multitudes followed Yeshua throughout His ministry, and after His resurrection, on the day of Pentecost alone, some three thousand came to the Lord. Ever since, whilst the disciples were permitted to preach in Judea, multiple tens of thousands were added to the faith. The headquarters of the Church was in Jerusalem, led by the Apostle James, the brother of Yeshua. (Acts 15:13). As the Apostles were sent out to the lost sheep of the house of Israel, they travelled to all the places around the Mediterranean Sea and beyond to discover where those reprobate sons of the covenant might be found. In the process, the word of the Gospel of the Kingdom, which spoke of the messianic restoration of the two houses of Israel into one United Kingdom, spread like wildfire among those Israelites in the diaspora. After an elapse of time these Gentile Israelites became the majority of the worldwide congregation, and upon the death of the apostles the worldly influence of Helenism began to infiltrate the body of Messiah. This is where it all began to go wrong, as in this the seeds of separation between Gentile and Jew found firm root. When the body of Messiah came under the influence of Greek culture, it began to reject the ways of Judah, which were those of the Torah contained in the Five Books of Moses. Judah then began to turn away from the truth of Yeshua.

The question is, what if – just what if Ephraim, the prodigal house of Israel, turned back to the Torah? What would happen between Judah and Ephraim? What would happen between Christian and Jew? The two faces of Israel would suddenly begin to recognise each other! Remember, the root word for witness means to DUPLICATE! The good witness 'duplicates' the Torah. To duplicate the Torah means you have to live it just like our Master Yeshua did when He walked on this earth. The Prophet Ezekiel shows us how the Christian and Jewish faces of Israel will come back together in the near future:

"As for you, son of man, take a stick for yourself and write on it: 'For Judah and for the children of Israel, his companions.' Then take another stick and write on it, 'For Joseph, the stick of Ephraim, and for all the house of Israel, his companions.' "Say to them, "This says the LORD GOD: "Surely I will take the stick of Joseph, which is in the hand

of Ephraim, and the tribes of Israel, his companions; and I will join them with it, with the stick of Judah, and make them one on My hand""
(Ezekiel 37:16&19, NKJV, emphasis added).

Some say that Joseph, i.e. Ephraim will become part of Judah and advocate that Christians should convert to Judaism. Others say that Judah will become part of Ephraim and convert to Christianity. This is not what the Scripture says! God says that Judah and Ephraim will become ONE in MY hand! The right hand of YHVH, the Holy One of Israel is Yeshua our Messiah. What this means is that it will take the hand of Yeshua to bring reconciliation and reunification between those two estranged houses of Israel. The question is, how will He do it? The Prophet Hosea provides us with the answer. As so often with prophetic pronouncements, it may not be the answer you want to hear, but it is the answer none the less:

"The pride of Israel testifies to his face; Therefore Israel and Ephraim stumble in their iniquity, Judah also stumbles with them. Therefore I will be to Ephraim like a moth, and to the house of Judah like rottenness." (Hosea 5:5&12, NKJV, emphasis added).

The message is that Ephraim and Judah, the two houses of Israel, composed of Christians on the one hand and Jews on the other, will find each other in the fires of the great tribulation. It is in the time described by the Prophet Jeremiah, as the *'time of Jacob's trouble'*, that Yeshua the Good Shepherd of Israel, will rescue and bring His people together and make them One in His hand. Both houses are full of pride and sin. Ephraim and Judah, the two faces of Israel, will stumble and fall before King Yeshua. It is only when they see the light, of the lamp that is Yeshua, the Word made flesh and the living Torah, that both parts of Israel will become reconciled to each other.

When we see our Savior Yeshua on one side, and the unity of the two houses of Israel on the other side, just think what can be accomplished when these two pillars are joined together in perfect unity. The Prophet Zechariah has a mighty comment about this, as these two Christian and Jewish sons of Israel finally defeat the spirit of Hellenism, which has divided them for so long:

"For I have bent Judah, My bow, fitted the bow with Ephraim, and raised up your sons, O Zion, against you O Greece, and made you like the sword of a mighty man. Then the LORD will be seen over them, and His arrow will go forth like lightning. The Lord GOD will blow the trumpet, and go with whirlwinds from the south."
(Zecheriah 9:13-14, NKJV, emphasis added).

Notice that both houses, Judah and Ephraim will be used by Yeshua, who is the archer, as only an archer can wield the bow. The sword is two-edged and it represents the Torah. The Hebrew root word for Torah is 'Yarah' which means to shoot straight to the mark, as in a target. When people sin, they miss the target. So, when will all of these things take place, and what will be the sign of His coming?

When will we know and what will be the sign of His coming?

If you have got this far and maintained an open mind along the way, having checked the Scriptures much like the Bereans of old, to see if these things be so, you will have had your eyes opened to the Gospel of the Kingdom, as preached throughout both the Old and the New [refreshed] Testament. Even after the resurrection of Yeshua, the disciples had heard

Him: *"Speaking of the things pertaining to the kingdom of God".* (Acts 1:3b). Consequently, having benefited from a further forty days of intensive teaching they asked the question that had been burning in their hearts:

"Lord, wilt thou at this time RESTORE AGAIN THE KINGDOM TO ISRAEL?" (Acts 1:6 KJV, emphasis added).

Yeshua answered them by saying: *"It is not for you to know times or seasons which the Father has put in His own authority"* (Acts 1:7 NKJV).

The truth is that the Kingdom will be restored to Israel! The reason it could not be restored in their day is because a number of prophesied events had yet to occur, such as the destruction of the second Temple, as well as the second expulsion of the Jews into the Diaspora. Furthermore, it could only take place after the Jews had returned once again in the end times to reestablish themselves in the Land of Promise. This event occurred with the founding of the State of Israel in 1948. Thus, today, for the first time in generations, nearly all the pieces are already in place to see the Kingdom of God established upon the earth. As we have already seen, there is only one thing that still needs to happen before His Kingdom can become a glorious reality.

Yeshua's disciples asked Him the question to which so many believers ever since have wanted to know the answer: *"And what will be the SIGN of Your coming* (Greek Perusia = Presence), *and of the end of the age?"*

Yeshua Himself gives us the final key: *"And THIS GOSPEL OF THE KINGDOM will be preached in all the world as a witness to all the nations, and then the end will come".* (Matthew 24:3b & 14 NKJV, emphasis added).

Therefore, when we see this Kingdom Gospel about the Restoration of the Whole House of Israel being preached throughout all the nations, THEN we know we are very close to the end of this age of human misrule. This is the key SIGN that the Age of Messiah is dawning!

There is a fascinating statement by Yeshua recorded for us in the Gospel of Matthew. It is a word that can only be understood in the light of our understanding that there are two houses of Israel, one centred on Judah, whilst the other is scattered throughout all the nations of the world. Just prior to this most significant word about the end time, He warns His disciples of the terrible persecution that is to come, and He encourages His disciples with: *"But he who endures to the end will be saved!"* Immediately after this, He goes on to make His remarkable statement:

"When they persecute you in this city, flee to another. For assuredly, I say to you, you will not have gone through THE CITIES OF ISRAEL before the Son of man comes". (Matthew 10:23, NKJV, emphasis added).

Is this not an incredible statement! Notice, it does not say, the cities of Judah! When we consider the State of Israel today, it would take a group of disciples less than a week to go through all the cities of Israel, as it is such a small country, with a Jewish population of barely six million. Clearly, Yeshua, the Good Shepherd, is speaking here about His end time servants, when both houses of Israel will be His Two Witnesses in the earth, together testifying and proclaiming that the Kingdom is at hand. Their ministry is so all encompassing, as they have to go to the four corners of the earth to all the cities of Israel, where the people of His flock have been scattered. Thus, Yeshua is saying that there will not be enough time for His servants to go through ALL the cities of Israel before He comes to establish His Kingdom on Mount Zion in Jerusalem, here upon the earth.

The two faces of Israel, the Christian and the Jew, are destined to come face to face and be reconciled with each other. Is it not highly ironic that whilst the face of Judah is easily recognized by the world, the face of Joseph/Ephraim is not? Yet, for those of us familiar with the story of Joseph, it should not surprise us, as Joseph's own brothers, when brought before him in Egypt, did not recognize him either. Just imagine, his own brothers did not recognize him, because he was dressed in Egyptian clothes, and besides this, they thought he was dead? Joseph's history, where no one, not even his own brothers recognised him, serves as a perfect analogy for the Lost House of Israel, which even to this day is also not recognized. They don't recognize it because, it too is dressed in Gentile clothes, and everybody thinks these tribes are dead also.

From the above material, we can see that our Heavenly Father is working out His purpose to bring a greater awareness of His plan for the restoration of His *Unified* Kingdom, not only to His chosen people in the camp of Judah, but also to His Christian children in Joseph's territory. Clearly, there is a long way to go, and still much remains to be done. However, we can take encouragement from the fact that all prophesies regarding His United Kingdom of Israel are set to be fulfilled. The prophets of the Bible forecast the ultimate future scenario for Joseph and his fellow Israelite tribesmen, as according to the prophets of Israel their destiny is to be reunited with their Jewish kinsmen of the tribe of Judah into one nation.

The prophet Ezekiel gave the most emphatic prophecy on the future reunion of Judah and Israel:

"Say to them, 'Thus says the LORD GOD, "Behold, I will gather Israel from among the nations where they have gone, and I will gather them from every side and bring them into their own land; and I will make them ONE NATION in the land, on the mountains of Israel; and one king will be king for all of them; and they will no longer be TWO NATIONS and no longer be divided into TWO KINGDOMS."
(Ezekiel 37:15-16, 19, 21-22 NASB, editor's emphasis).

This is the messianic age the Bible speaks of – an age of true peace, when finally, *'swords shall be turned into ploughshares and spears into pruning hooks.'*

Finally, I would like to end by quoting a poem, which was written by a ten year old boy c. 1940, whilst in a ghetto in Poland. The boy has long since died in one of Hitler's gas chambers, but his words live on to haunt us and also to warn us. I believe the words of this nameless Jewish boy contain a prophetic message for us Christians and Jews – the two faces of Israel today. As you read the words below, just imagine that Messiah Yeshua is speaking to you personally.

"I am Israel, the home of Abraham, Isaac and Jacob,

I am the home of the children of Jacob,

I am Israel, waiting for my children to return from Egypt,

I am the Israel, of Saul, David and Jonathan,

I am Israel and I withstood the wrath of the Babylonians,

In Babylonia my children dreamed and their dream still lives.

I am Israel and I heard Cyrus sound the first return to Zion,

I am Israel and I withstood the pillage of the Romans, and I cried at the

sacrifice of Masada. I am Israel and I saw them send my children away,

I am Israel and I wait to embrace my children once again,

I am Israel and I see the storm beginning on the horizon,

and I see my children in the yoke of the oppressor, as in the days of old,

I am Israel and I want my children, and when they are with me again,

I want to take them to my bosom and they will be forever free!"

"FOR I AM ISRAEL!"

BIBLIOGRAPHY

A DIFFERENT GOD? – Reassessing The Place of Israel and The Church in God's Story, by Dr. Dwight A Pryor, published by CFI Charitable Trust, England, 2007.

ANTIQUITIES OF THE JEWS, by Flavius Josephus, translated by William Whiston A.M., London.

BABYLON IN EUROPE: What Bible Prophecy Reveals About The European Union, by David Hathaway, published by, New Wine Press, United Kingdom

BEYOND BABYLON: Europe's Rise and Fall, by David Ben Ariel, published by Publish America, LLLP, Baltimore, U.S.A. 2004.

COMPLETE JEWISH BIBLE, Translation by David Stern, published by Jewish New Testament Publications, Inc, Clarksville, Maryland USA.

DANIEL DERONDA: by George Elliot, published by Wordsworth Editions Limited, Ware, Herts, England, 1996.

FOR THE LOVE OF ZION – Christian witness and the restoration of Israel, by Kelvin Crombie, published by Hodder & Stoughton, London, Great Britain.

HAS THE LAW BEEN NAILED TO THE CROSS? By Stephen J Spykerman, published by Mayim Chayim Messianic Community, England, 2000.

IN DEFENCE OF ISRAEL: The Bible's Mandate for supporting the Jewish State, by John Hagee, published by, Front Line – A Strang Company, Florida, U.S.A.

ISRAEL'S FEASTS and their FULLNESS, by Batya Ruth Wootten, published by Key of David Publishing, St Cloud, FL USA, 2002.

ISRAEL'S TRIBES TODAY, by Steven M Collins, published by Bible Blessings, Royal Oak, MI, U.S.A. 2005.

JESUS WAS A JEW, by Dr. Arnold G Fruchtenbaum, published by Ariel Ministries Press, Tustin, California, U.S.A.

MEAT IN DUE SEASON, by J G Messervy-Norman, Second Edition, published by LuLu, USA, 2006.

NEW AMERICAN STANDARD BIBLE, published by Zondervan, Grand Rapids, Michigan, USA, 2002.

OBSERVATIONS UPON THE PROPHECIES OF DANIEL AND THE APOCALYPSE OF ST JOHN, by Sir Isaac Newton, London, England 1733, re- published by Nuvision Publications, LLC, 2007.

ORIGIN – You too are from Israel – You too are the People, by Yair Davidiy, published by Russell-Davis Publishers, Jerusalem, Israel, 2002.

RESTORING THE JEWISHNESS OF THE GOSPEL – A Message for Christians, by David H Stern, Jewish New Testament Publications, Clarksville, MD, USA.

SIX DAYS and a DAY – The Creator's Blueprint to Make Us Like Jesus, by Martin Byers, published by Destiny Image Publishers, Shippensburg, PA, USA.

THE CHUMASH – THE ARTSCROLL SERIES/STONE EDITION, published by Mesorah Publications, Ltd., Brooklyn, NY, U.S.A. 1993.

THE EXHAUSTIVE CONCORDANCE OF THE BIBLE, by James Strong, published by Mac Donald Publishing Company, McLean, Virginia, U.S.A.

THE HEBREW YESHUA VS. THE GREEK JESUS, by Nehemiah Gordon, published by Hilkiah Press, Jerusalem, Israel, 2005.

THE HIDDEN ANCESTRY OF AMERICA AND GREAT BRITAIN, by Stephen Spykerman., published by Mount Ephraim Publishing, England, 2004.

THE HOLY BIBLE, King James Version, published by Oxford University Press, London, Great Britain.

THE PROPHECIES OF ABRAHAM, by Joseph F Dumond, published by Author House, England, 2010.

THE RIGHTS OF THE KINGDOM, by John Sadler, Printed by Richard Bishop, London, England, 1649.

THE STONE EDITION TANACH, PUBLISHED BY Mesorah Publications Ltd, New York, USA, Second Edition 1998.

THE TRIBES – The Israelite Origins of Western Peoples, by Yair Davidiy, Third Edition, - Russell-Davis Publishers, Jerusalem, Israel 2004.

WHAT'S THE MESSIAH WAITING FOR? By John Hulley, unpublished manuscript, Israel 2005.

"WHO ARE YOU, AMERICA? – TIME TO LIFT YOUR PROPHETIC VEIL" By Stephen Spykerman, published by Mount Ephraim Publishing, 2nd edition, England, 2010.

YOU DON'T HAVE TO BE JEWISH TO BE A ZIONIST – A Review of 400 years of Christian Zionism, by Eliyahu Tal, published by; A Millenium Publication of the International Forum for a United Jerusalem, Israel.

Unless stated otherwise, all Scriptural references are from the New King James Version, - Copyright 1982, Thomas Nelson Inc. Emphases are the author's.

ABOUT THE AUTHOR

STEPHEN J SPYKERMAN was born the fourth son of a Dutch father and an English mother in September 1940 during the Nazi occupation of Holland. Having received a solid general education, he spurned the higher education his parents had hoped for him and entered the world of retail fashion at age nineteen. A few years later he moved to London, where he trained as a tailor in various high-class fashion houses. Whilst he was aware that his maternal grandfather had been a renowned tailor in London, he did not realise at the time that he was following a family tradition going back for at least five generations. He met his future wife Virginia, who was a colleague at the fashion house where they were both employed, and one day they attended a Billy Graham Crusade in London. On the second visit they gave their lives to the Lord and started attending Westminster Chapel, where they were being taught by the great Dr Martyn Lloyd-Jones, the renowned evangelical author and Bible teacher. Then in 1965 he married Virginia Edwards, and soon afterwards they moved out of London to East Anglia. Whilst there, the couple earnestly sought the strong meat of solid Bible teaching they had become accustomed to, but could not find it anywhere in their new location. It was whilst Stephen was searching, that his eyes were being opened to the Hebrew roots of the

Christian faith. In 1970, at age 30, both he and his wife were baptised by full immersion in a Sabbath keeping church. At age 40 he was ordained a Deacon and after a long interval of dedicated service at age 60 he was ordained an Elder in a thriving Messianic Community in England. Stephen now plans to return to Israel, the Land of his fathers, on his 70th birthday together with his wife and daughter.

After the second of his four children was born, he left the fashion industry to take up a more lucrative career in financial services. During a successful career, he pioneered a number of new schemes and concepts in charitable giving and gave investment seminars. He became an international speaker in his field and his interest in public speaking led him to direct his own public speaking club. In the years prior to his retirement in 1997, he became involved in an International Speakers Bureau, after which he and a colleague set up a similar Speakers Bureau at Kew Gardens in London.

Once retired from day to day business, he founded Mount Ephraim Publishing. He started writing books and published numerous articles. To this day he continues to write and give lectures around the world. Stephen Spykerman is a dynamic speaker who has addressed numerous audiences, both large and small, in conferences in England, the United States, Ireland, France, Belgium, the Netherlands, Israel, Malta and Cyprus.

"CHRISTIANS & JEWS – *The Two Faces of Israel!"*- is the authors sixth book to date, and it contains a most dramatic and eye-opening insight into the hidden meaning behind many of the Parables and the Miracles of the Gospels. The author opens up the story behind the origins of Christian Zionism and examines the mysteries of the latest move of the Spirit which has brought about the worldwide Hebrew Roots movement.

BY THE SAME AUTHOR:

"HAS THE LAW BEEN NAILED TO THE CROSS?
Is there a conflict between the Law of the Old Testament and the Gospel of the New Testament?
Published by: MAYIM CHAYIM MESSIANIC COMMUNITY, England, 2002

"GREAT BRITAIN - HER CALLING AND HIDDEN ANCESTRY"
Published by: MOUNT EPHRAIM PUBLISHING, England, 2004

"THE HIDDEN ANCESTRY OF AMERICA AND GREAT BRITAIN"
Published by: MOUNT EPHRAIM PUBLISHING, England, 2005

"WHO ARE YOU, AMERICA? – TIME TO LIFT YOUR PROPHETIC VEIL, Published by: MOUNT EPHRAIM PUBLISHING, England, 2005, 2nd Edition; 2010

"AMERICA'S THIRD PERIL– A PROPHECY WHO'S TIME HAS COME!" Published by AUTHOR HOUSE, Bloomington, IN 47403, U.S.A., 2010

CPSIA information can be obtained at www.ICGtesting.com
Printed in the USA
LVOW07s0901041015

456838LV00002B/222/P